THE ART OF CONCEALMENT

Giles Cole

THE ART OF CONCEALMENT

OBERON BOOKS
LONDON

WWW.OBERONBOOKS.COM

First published in 2012 by Oberon Books Ltd
521 Caledonian Road, London N7 9RH
Tel: +44 (0) 20 7607 3637 / Fax: +44 (0) 20 7607 3629
e-mail: info@oberonbooks.com
www.oberonbooks.com

PB ISBN: 978-1-84943-416-4
Digital ISBN: 978-1-84943-547-5

Photograph courtesy of Princess George Galitzine (Jean Dawnay);
image design by Clare Martin, Topaz Digital Media.

Visit www.oberonbooks.com to read more about all our books
and to buy them. You will also find features, author interviews and
news of any author events, and you can sign up for e-newsletters
so that you're always first to hear about our new releases.

Characters

OLDER TERRY

YOUNGER TERRY

CUTHBERT WORSLEY
early 40s – late 50s

FRANK RATTIGAN
early 40s – mid-50s

FREDDIE GILMOUR
mid-40s – mid-50s

VERA RATTIGAN
late 40s – early 70s

AUNT EDNA
indeterminate middle age

KENNETH MORGAN
early 20s – late 20s

MICHAEL FRANKLIN
early 20s – mid-40s

TONY GOLDSCHMIDT
18

Chronologically, there is a wide span of years and ages, but except where indicated in the text, characters should not take too much trouble to try and look a particular age in a particular scene. They all appear as Older Terry remembers or imagines them to look, and precise age is immaterial.

The roles of Frank Rattigan and Freddie Gilmour, as well as Vera Rattigan and Aunt Edna, can be doubled; Kenneth and Michael can also be doubled, or even trebled with Tony; this would allow the ten roles to be played by six or seven actors, as well as creating some interesting resonances between the doubled roles.

The people and events portrayed in this play are based on certain known biographical facts, but the play is, first and foremost, a work of imagination. Specifically, the character of Freddie Gilmour is an invention – but an invention inspired by several of Rattigan's friends and colleagues.

Setting

Although there are various locations throughout the play, the setting can be very simple, with a minimum of furniture. A chaise-longue or sofa, two small armchairs or other seating, a small desk and a drinks cabinet would suffice. All scenes are recalled in Older Terry's memory, and the action of the play can therefore appear to take place in an abstract space, defined simply by the furnishings and props and occasional sound effects.

Musical links between scenes are envisaged, but not obligatory.

Acknowledgements
Amongst various other sources, the biographies of Rattigan – *Terence Rattigan – A Biography* by Geoffrey Wansell (Oberon Books) and *Terence Rattigan – The Man and His Work* by Michael Darlow (Quartet) – were both invaluable reading.

The Art of Concealment was first opened at the Iambic Arts Theatre, Brighton, in May 2011, as part of the Brighton Festival Fringe, and to mark the centenary of Rattigan's birth. It was directed by Tom Latter, with Robert Rowe, Kieran Gough, Gay Soper, Guy Warren-Thomas, Graham Pountney, Christopher Morgan and Sam Harding in the cast.

A new production opened at the Jermyn Street Theatre, London, in January 2012. It was presented by John B. Hobbs and Alexander Marshall in association with Jermyn Street Theatre and GC Productions. The director was Knight Mantell, and the designer Meg Witts, with lighting by Howard Hudson, sound by Andrew Johnson and incidental music by MattGray Sound. The cast was as follows:

OLDER TERRY	Alistair Findlay
YOUNGER TERRY	Dominic Tighe
CUTHBERT WORSLEY	Christopher Morgan
FRANK / FREDDIE	Graham Pountney
VERA / AUNT EDNA	Judy Buxton
KENNETH MORGAN	Daniel Bayle
MICHAEL FRANKLIN	Charlie Hollway
TONY GOLDSCHMIDT	Benedict Salter

The play then transferred to Riverside Studios, Hammersmith, in May 2012, with the following cast changes:

OLDER TERRY	Brian Deacon
YOUNGER TERRY	Ashley Cook
CUTHBERT WORSLEY	Oliver Hume
TONY / KENNETH / MICHAEL	Ewan Goddard

The lighting designer at Riverside Studios was Gary Bowman, and costumes were by Jackie Crier at Masquerade.

Act One

A blank space which will later become the Royal Box at Her Majesty's Theatre, Haymarket. Music is heard from a distance, then subsides.

Spot on OLDER TERRY. He is wearing a dinner jacket and is leaning heavily on a walking stick. He has a glass of whisky in his other hand.

OLDER TERRY: The fact is I'm dying. And why shouldn't a man enjoy his own death? After all, it's the last amusement left. They got the diagnosis wrong last time. It wasn't leukaemia, but it is now. Second time unlucky. *(Drinks.)* Shouldn't be drinking this, but have to steady the nerves. I have a terror of opening nights and tonight is no exception. *(He sits, carefully.)*

Despite many protestations to the contrary by my friends – and indeed by myself from time to time – I am coming to the conclusion that I am not a nice man. I do, however, though I say it myself, have some rather fine qualities. One or two. I am loyal, in my own way. And I... well, I'm loyal anyway. Buggered up a lot of things, let's be frank.

I made money, of course. That always helps. But I spent far, far too much of it. Drove several accountants to despair. No, don't exaggerate. Drove one accountant to despair. 'Don't give so many lavish parties, Mr Rattigan. Don't buy that house, Mr Rattigan, you don't need another one. And for goodness' sake stop gambling.' All to no avail. What's money for if not to have fun? I've been generous – if you can call that a fine quality. I like giving presents. Simple fact. And people like receiving them. Not so easy to give affection, though. Love. Bit more of a mystery, that one.

I'm 66 years old and my looks have gone. They went a long time ago – somewhere between 1958 and 1960.

(Laughs briefly.) I am no longer the Prettiest Playwright in London. Not by a long chalk. But I am still a playwright. I have always been a playwright, above and beyond anything else. Even when I was at school. Oh God, I've resisted these memories.

Perhaps we see, for a moment, half-lit in the background, the shadowy figures of FRANK, VERA, TONY, CUTHBERT and YOUNGER TERRY.

It feels like giving in, to think back to your happier days. But now is the time. I can resist no longer. *(Drinks.)* Where are you, young Terence? Are you still hiding somewhere in my past? Come on out, then, and face me. Come out and torture me, before my last play starts.

A short piece of music is heard. Lights up on YOUNGER TERRY. He is handsome, debonair, and stands in a very casual and relaxed pose, cigarette in hand. The other characters disappear and the OLDER and YOUNGER TERRY regard each other for a moment.

God, just look at you. Handsome young bastard.

YOUNGER TERRY exhales and smiles, with the natural confidence of youth.

So proud of yourself. So self-assured. Such a noble confection.

TERRY: Aren't I just?

OLDER TERRY: How did you get away with it?

TERRY: Practice, old man. Practice. Surely you can't have forgotten?

Lights down on OLDER TERRY.

Music.

SCENE TWO. 1929.

TERRY's study at Harrow. Afternoon.

YOUNGER TERRY remains in the same position. The voice of FRANK RATTIGAN, Terry's father, can be heard approaching.

FRANK: *(Off.)* My dear young chap, if you are a sporting type, you are a sporting type, and it's as simple as that.

FRANK enters, followed by TONY GOLDSCHMIDT.

FRANK cuts a dashing figure – he is well-groomed, with a neat moustache, and is wearing a sporty jacket with a cravat at his neck and a carnation in his buttonhole. He is a little tipsy, but is accustomed to holding his drink. TONY is slightly built, fresh-faced and somewhat tongue-tied in company. He is wearing formal school uniform, and is carrying a boater. He is clearly in awe of FRANK, to TERRY's annoyance.

FRANK: I may have had my moments – and I flatter myself I was somewhat prolific in that department – but, as Terence will tell you, my life has not been a bed of roses.

In Cairo, one could play any game one liked – polo, cricket, golf, tennis, squash racquets and croquet. Anything that took your fancy.

TONY: Did you play all of them, sir?

FRANK: At one time or another, yes. Mostly stuck to cricket and tennis, though. That's where I excelled. Terence is the same. Takes after me, don't you, Terry? Damn good eye. I'll be expecting to see you opening the batting against Eton, my boy.

TERRY: That is a distinct possibility.

FRANK: A distinct possibility! Do you hear the way he talks? They'll pick you, my boy, and no mistake about it. If there's a Rattigan at the school, he'll be picked for the Eton match. Have you been to Lord's for the match, Goldschmidt?

TONY: No, sir, I'm afraid not. It's not really my –

FRANK: Oh, you should, you should. Shouldn't he, Terence? It's a great occasion. Thousands of people, all dressed up fit to kill. Quite a fashion parade, I can assure you.

TONY: It sounds very – (glamorous).

FRANK: Now then, what refreshment can you offer us, my boy?

TERRY: We aren't allowed alcohol in our studies, Father.

FRANK: Really? Then what's the point of being a monitor?

TERRY: I am not a monitor.

FRANK: Not? Why not? You a Rattigan and not a monitor – what's wrong with the old place? *(He laughs.)*

TERRY: Anyway, I'd have thought you'd have had enough at lunch.

A beat. FRANK assimilates this.

TONY: Very good lunch, sir. Thank you.

FRANK: Not at all. My pleasure to treat my son. And his friend. By the way, don't call me sir.

TONY: Oh –

FRANK: Major will do.

TERRY catches TONY's eye, raises his eyes to heaven.

Pity you aren't a sporting fellow, Goldschmidt. We might have had more to talk about.

TERRY: You could have talked about Catullus. Or Seneca. Or Ancient Rome in general.

FRANK: Don't try and be smart with me, boy.

TERRY: I'm merely pointing out that they are Tony's areas of expertise. You could have asked him about something he knows.

TONY: I am a bit of a classicist, that's true, Major.

FRANK: Most laudable, I'm sure. Beats me how you two get on. Not buggers, are you?

A beat.

TERRY: Oh, Father, please.

FRANK: There's a lot of it goes on in some schools. Wouldn't be surprised if there weren't a few buggers even at Harrow. *(Marches to the window.)* Damn good view from your study, Terence. See the place in all its glory, eh? Did you know that if you could see that far, you could see St Petersburg from here?

TERRY: Father, if we could see that far, we could see China.

TONY: Actually, that is quite a logical statement.

FRANK: *(Ignoring this)* So. Happy here, are you?

TERRY: Does it matter if I'm not?

FRANK: What kind of a remark is that?

TERRY: *(Lightly)* It's simply a question.

A pause. FRANK feels less sure of himself.

FRANK: Goldschmidt, I assume you're not a drinking man?

TONY: I'm afraid not. I've never quite got the hang of it. I tried a Gin and It once, and it didn't agree with me. I was really quite ill. I think I might have an allergy –

FRANK: Goldschmidt, my boy, you just haven't lived.

TONY: No, sir – Major.

FRANK holds his gaze, willing him to leave.

FRANK: I *would* like a private conversation with my son, if it's all the same to you.

TONY: Oh. Yes. Sorry. I – well – perhaps I ought to be moving along, actually…

FRANK: Pleasure meeting you.

TONY: Sorry – I didn't mean to blather on about drinking.

FRANK: Not at all.

TONY: I always do that when I'm in company. Blather on, I mean. Or else I say nothing at all, which probably seems equally rude. Sorry. I've greatly enjoyed meeting you, Major. And thank you again for lunch.

FRANK waves a hand, dismissively.

I'll – erm – yes. Be on my way.

TERRY: Dicabimus laxus, meus amicus.

TONY: Acquiesco. Pater tuus personam coloratum est.

TONY goes.

FRANK: What atrocious Latin. 'Your father is a colourful person' indeed!

TERRY: It was a kind of joke. Because Tony's so hot at all that we speak deliberate schoolboy stuff. We find it amusing.

FRANK: Look. Terence. I know I've not been the most attentive of fathers…

TERRY holds his gaze, expectantly.

But I would like to have a word.

TERRY: Ah. Man to man stuff.

FRANK: You're angry with me. I can tell.

TERRY: All those years in the Diplomatic Service weren't wasted then.

FRANK: I shall ignore that. Look, I want to speak candidly to you.

TERRY: Well, clearly something's up. Otherwise you would have a little blonde number on your arm, as usual. I've never known a man have so many young female cousins.

FRANK: They're just…company. That's all. Your mother doesn't like gallivanting around all over the place, and –

TERRY: And you do.

FRANK: Yes. I do. I am what people sometimes call a social butterfly. I flit about, here, there and everywhere. It's just the way I am.

TERRY: And you flit better in female company…

A beat.

FRANK: All right, have your jibes if you must. I'm trying to be honest with you. Sit down, boy, sit down, there's a good fellow.

TERRY sits.

To the point. Constantinople.

TERRY: What about it?

FRANK: My disagreement with Lord Curzon. British policy toward the Turks. Et cetera.

TERRY: Yes?

FRANK: Cost me my career. Cost me a knighthood.

TERRY: Yes, Father, I know.

FRANK: The point is – that was the official story. The story I told everybody at the time. But I want to tell you the real story. You're a fine young chap now, Terence, just like I was, and…this isn't easy for me…I want you to…I want you to avoid the mistakes I have made.

TERRY: Are you telling me there was some kind of scandal?

FRANK: I am not proud of myself, you must understand that, first and foremost. I have been foolish in my time. Very foolish. I was conducting an amour in Constantinople. God help me, that was serious enough, but the person I chose to conduct it with… Madness. Utter madness.

TERRY: *(Suspecting a confession of homosexuality)* And this person was…somebody rather important, I presume?

FRANK: Precisely. Good God, I was young, full-blooded… I took my opportunities.

TERRY: I see. Yes. *(A beat.)* Are you going to tell me who this person was?

FRANK: It was the Princess Elisabeth of Romania.

TERRY: Oh. Oh, I see. I thought for a moment…

FRANK: And she then went and married the King of Greece. Who was not best pleased to discover that his wife had been having an affair with a foreign diplomat.

TERRY: How did he find out?

FRANK: She was pregnant.

TERRY: Ah. Well. That's… (different).

FRANK: Foreign Office took a dim view, had to appease the King, and so on and so forth. Resignation required. Career gone in a puff of smoke.

TERRY: Yes, I see.

FRANK: But the disgrace, Terry. That was the thing. I couldn't face the disgrace of being sacked for…for, well, being young and stupid. I still can't understand how it happened.

TERRY: The affair?

FRANK: I was always so careful. Used a double-layer device – you know – protective. God alone knows how she managed to get pregnant. Most unfortunate. Altogether. So. You see. Heed the warning, my boy. Always – always, without fail – use some kind of protection with the ladies – and make damn sure it works! That's my advice to you. Your brother went the same way with that laundry maid –

TERRY: Yes, naughty Brian.

FRANK: – and I don't want it to happen to you too.

TERRY: No, Father. I shall do my best to ensure that it doesn't. You have my word.

FRANK: *(Greatly relieved now.)* Good man. Good man. Well. Glad I've got that off my chest. So. Oxford next, eh?

TERRY: How is mother?

FRANK: Oh – well, well. Yes, she's…well.

TERRY: Good. Give her my love.

FRANK: I shall, I shall. I shall bring her to see you play for the Eleven against Eton.

TERRY: Provided I'm picked.

FRANK: Of course you'll be picked. You've got style. The Rattigan style. *(He mimes an expansive cover drive.)* Anyway. Look. Don't let my tales put you off the Diplomatic. It's a good career. A good life. You'll see the world.

TERRY: And meet princesses.

FRANK: Very good. Nice little joke, Terence. But look – just between you and me, eh? Don't want a story like that to… well, find the wrong ears. If you understand me. Keep it to ourselves, eh?

TERRY: Does Mother know?

FRANK: Good heavens, no. She's still on rather friendly terms with Queen Marie. Don't want to jeopardise that.

TERRY: Of course. That would be most unfair. One needs to be careful about the things one reveals.

FRANK: Just so. Discretion. That's the ticket.

An awkward pause. FRANK wants to say goodbye with a gesture of affection, but it doesn't come easily to him. He goes to TERRY and embraces him, clumsily. TERRY barely reacts. FRANK holds onto him for a fraction longer than is entirely comfortable for either of them, then steps back.

FRANK: Been good seeing you, my boy.

TERRY: You too, Father.

FRANK: I'll be off then.

TERRY: Righto.

Spot on OLDER TERRY. He is standing, leaning heavily on his stick, watching them.

OLDER TERRY: What my father never knew was that even then, when I was at Harrow, I, like him, had already embarked on a dangerous affair. In my case with a much older man. It was not only dangerous, it was foolhardy, and tremendously exciting. And therefore to be kept entirely under wraps. My own private little landscape. The pattern of my life was already set.

Lights fade on OLDER TERRY.

Music.

SCENE THREE. 1933.

The Rattigan family home, Stanhope Gardens, South Kensington. Morning.

VERA enters with a coffee tray, sets it down. She has a fragile beauty although now very much in her middle years. She is wearing a smart housecoat over her dress. She is a woman who sees genuine achievement in her position as the wife of a former diplomat.

YOUNGER TERRY enters, in blazer and flannels, greets her warmly with a kiss.

VERA: Your father is not best pleased, dear.

TERRY: I imagine not.

VERA pours coffee and hands him a cup.

VERA: I've done my best to placate him, but I've rarely seen him so enraged.

TERRY: Mother, I have to fight my own battles now.

She touches his face affectionately.

VERA: I know, dear. But I do worry about you.

TERRY: There's no need.

VERA: What it is to be the mother of two headstrong boys…

TERRY: Brian has only ever done what Father wanted. Tried to be another version of him. Another heroic Rattigan.

VERA: Terence, that isn't fair.

TERRY: Whereas I have simply decided to go my own way.

FRANK enters. He has a glass of whisky in his hand. He surveys them all.

VERA: Coffee, dear?

FRANK: *(To TERRY, ignoring this.)* I ought to strike you, sir.

TERRY: Sir? Who's 'sir'?

FRANK: Call yourself a son of mine?

TERRY: Not often, actually, no.

FRANK: You lead a life of privilege, bought by the sweat of my brow –

TERRY: Oh, please.

FRANK: You have all the advantages, and this is how you thank me.

TERRY: Father, I have done no more, and no less, than both Brian and yourself before me –

FRANK: It was an act of sheer effrontery! Not illness, not fear of failure – you deliberately fail even to turn up! For your *Finals*! You could have got a First. And you deliberately throw it all away – for what? I fail to understand you.

TERRY: I know.

FRANK: You think you're better than all of us, do you?

TERRY: That rather depends in what regard, Father.

FRANK: Do you hear the insolence of the boy, Vera?

Unable to make a useful contribution, VERA simply bows her head and waits for him to finish his tirade.

The way he talks so glibly, so patronisingly, as if we were simply journeymen clerks, or a firm of undertakers!

VERA: Frank, dear, please calm down. Let's talk about this rationally.

FRANK: You think I'm not being rational? My own wife thinks I'm not being rational?

VERA: That's not what I said.

FRANK: And what is young Terence going to make of himself now? Now that he's thrown his education in our faces. Well?

TERRY: *(Coolly.)* I'm going to try my hand at playwriting, Father. You need no degree for that. You simply need skill and imagination. And application, of course.

FRANK: Terence, it seems to me you are determined to live in a cloud-cuckoo-land. Acting out a few little scenes for fun – or writing a few little frivolities for your own amusement – those are harmless enough – but one grows out of that kind of foolery!

VERA: Frank, I do believe he has a talent for –

FRANK: What do you know about it? What do you know about talent? And play-acting?

VERA: I'm not saying I'm the best judge –

TERRY: Father, do please stop taking this out on Mother. It has nothing to do with her.

FRANK: Oh really? Well, who else has been filling your head with all these absurd fantasies?

VERA: I have simply done my best to encourage both our sons in whatever ways have seemed appropriate. You have seen to it that they both became excellent sportsmen – very well, that is as it should be. But it's a mother's duty to nurture what lies within.

FRANK: Damn it, Vera, writing plays just isn't a proper pursuit for a man! He should have a career, a position in life –

TERRY: Even if he throws away that position by behaving like a schoolboy?

A beat.

FRANK: I warn you, Terence –

TERRY: Yes?

FRANK: I warn you…not to try my patience any further.

TERRY: I shall do my best, but your patience does rather have a will of its own.

FRANK: Damn you and your smart answers! Do you take me for a fool? Do you?

TERRY: No, Father.

FRANK: Then kindly do me the courtesy of explaining what it is about 'plays' that fascinates you so much.

TERRY: The fact that they aren't real, but that they can contain more reality about human nature than almost anything else. It's a powerful thing to create something that people will watch, and listen to, and believe in for an hour or two, as if it were their own world, or a world with which they can choose to identify. It beats family arguments any day.

FRANK: But that's just it – you said it yourself. They aren't real! All they amount to is a…a group of people with painted faces parading around trying to be witty.

TERRY: That's rather a narrow view, if I may say so.

FRANK: I speak as I find.

TERRY: Clearly. But others find differently, Father. Surely you can accept that? Others find kinship, and…fellow feeling, a sharing of experience which…moves them. And helps them to step outside themselves for a brief time, before they resume the mundane task of going about their ordinary business.

FRANK: But it's not a proper job! For all you say, it's not a proper job.

TERRY: It could be. I could make it one.

VERA: I believe you could.

Pause. FRANK sits, tiredly.

I think what we have to accept, Frank, is that Terence feels he has a vocation –

FRANK: A what?

VERA: You heard me. And I think that whereas Brian wants to go into the law –

FRANK: Taking his time over that too. Hardly the brightest star in the legal firmament.

VERA: These things don't happen overnight, Frank. Now, as I was saying, for Brian it's the law – which is admirable, and happens to accord with your own view of the world – but for Terence it's the theatre, which, for the moment, *doesn't* accord with your view. But I think we should give him his chance. He was very involved in drama at Oxford – especially that production of *Romeo and Juliet*, with John Gielgud –

FRANK: Who?

VERA: He's very well-known, Frank. And I think the whole experience sparked things off inside Terence which could turn out to be quite wonderful.

TERRY: Thank you, Mother.

FRANK: Never did understand the appeal of Shakespeare.

VERA: That, dear, is neither here nor there.

TERRY: The thing about Shakespeare, Father, is that he is actually more important to us, to England, even than cricket.

FRANK: *(Appalled.)* What?

TERRY: He may not be to everyone's taste – but he created a body of work that will outlive every generation.

FRANK: So you think you can be another Shakespeare, do you?

TERRY: Certainly not. But if I can write one play that might still be read or performed in fifty years' time, I shall have achieved something. And if I had to choose between the same profession as Shakespeare and – let us say – the Diplomatic Service, I would follow Shakespeare every time.

FRANK: And what is so wrong with the Diplomatic Service?

TERRY: I'm sure it has its uses, but it exists within its own tight-knit little world which has little relevance to the vast majority of –

FRANK: On the contrary, it's the perfect way in which to see the world and understand other people.

TERRY: Yes, but what do they add up to, seriously, all those postings here, there and everywhere – apart from some damn good sporting opportunities?

FRANK: A KCMG usually.

VERA: *(Taking this as a shaft of humour.)* Oh, Frank…

FRANK: Not in my case, however. But that's another story – which we shan't go into now. You, though – you could do it, Terence. You could get a KCMG.

TERRY: I can't go through life trying to make up for the things that eluded you, Father. I'm sorry. I can't.

They lock eyes for a moment. FRANK drinks.

FRANK: So. Where does this leave us?

VERA: I suggest that we give Terence his chance – but with a time limit. Let him have a year, two years, to try and make a go of things, and if at the end of that period he hasn't managed to do so, then we'll think again.

FRANK: And meanwhile I support him, is that it?

VERA: He is your son, dear, when all's said and done.

Pause. FRANK knows he is beaten.

FRANK: *(Sighs.)* Very well. £200 a year for two years. After that you take any job that I can find for you. Diplomatic or otherwise.

TERRY looks at VERA. She smiles.

TERRY: Agreed. Thank you. Thank you, Mother.

VERA exits.

FRANK: Just…um, don't get yourself into any trouble. You know what I mean.

TERRY: You won't hear a whiff of scandal.

FRANK looks at him, levelly.

FRANK: Glad to hear it. Well. I suppose I'd better wish you good luck.

TERRY: Thank you.

FRANK: Drink?

TERRY: Why not?

FRANK: Good man.

They turn to go. FRANK exits.

Spot on OLDER TERRY.

OLDER TERRY: I was 22 years old and obnoxious.

TERRY: Obnoxious? That's a little harsh.

OLDER TERRY: I thought myself witty and stylish. Quite the entertainer. Had them in stitches at Oxford.

TERRY: 'Lady Diana Coutigan'. Such a grande dame. It was a bravura performance, even if I say so myself.

OLDER TERRY: Yes, you always said so yourself.

YOUNGER TERRY smiles at him and goes.

I may have appeared frivolous, but I knew my own mind. There was always an audience in my head, and because there was an audience, I performed. I wrote six, seven plays one after the other – including one with poor tongue-tied Tony Goldschmidt – and sent them off in turn to all the London managements. And, one after another, they all came back. Finally, one of them softened the blow by asking to see something else of mine. I only had two possibilities left. I wanted to send a turgid drama, but my mother parcelled up a lightweight piece of fluff called *Joie de Vivre,* based on my experiences in a crammer in France. The management suddenly had to fill a theatre for a few weeks and in desperation they turned to my play. And *Joie de Vivre* became *French Without Tears.* Against all odds it was a massive hit and ran for over a thousand performances. I can still hear the cheers. Even to this day.

I can't deny that the abdication crisis probably helped the box office. But I had my start. I was up and running. You could say I owed it all to my mother and to Mrs Wallis Simpson.

Struggled after that. Not so easy to have a second hit. So I joined the RAF and went hunting for German submarines. Liked the uniform. Suited me.

Lights fade on OLDER TERRY.

Music.

SCENE FOUR. 1942.

An ante-room to a private box at the Apollo Theatre, Shaftesbury Avenue. Evening.

A background buzz of the audience leaving the theatre. VERA is very elegantly dressed in a full evening gown and stole and carrying a programme for 'Flare Path'. After a moment, YOUNGER TERRY appears, in RAF uniform. VERA puts on her best smile and turns to him, motioning him to sit with her. He does so.

VERA: We're very proud of you, Terence.

TERRY: You mean *you* are. *(He kisses her on the cheek.)*

VERA: No, your father too. I told him he should say so, but you know what he's like. Can't come out with a straightforward statement if it involves any kind of decent feeling. He's gone to fetch some drinks instead.

TERRY: He's on much safer ground there.

VERA: *(Laughs.)* I'm afraid so. But it's true. We are both very proud.

TERRY: It's all down to you, Mother.

VERA: Don't be so silly.

TERRY: If it weren't for you I'd probably be a junior clerk in some government outpost.

VERA: Nonsense. Not a word to your father, though. He doesn't know that I had any hand in it at all – and he doesn't need to know.

CUTHBERT announces himself with a discreet cough. He is a man doomed to look middle-aged before his time, ungainly of physique, and wearing spectacles and an ill-fitting dinner suit. He suffers from emphysema, which gives his voice a slight breathy quality, but this should only become really noticeable in later scenes when he is older and the condition more pronounced.

Ah, Cuthbert, there you are. Wasn't it splendid?

CUTHBERT: It certainly was, Mrs R. And the Air Ministry thinks so too. In fact, Terry, I am bidden to invite you for a drink with the Chief of the Air Staff himself, Sir Charles Portal. He wants to be the first to congratulate you. He's waiting for you in his box.

TERRY: Then I'd better attend.

CUTHBERT: You certainly had. And there's a whole line of top brass waiting to shake your hand after he's finished with you. Excuse us, Mrs R.

Just as they turn to go, FRANK appears, with three glasses of champagne. He is wearing full evening dress.

FRANK: Oh, Terence. Got you a glass.

TERRY: Sorry, Father. Have to go and shake a few hands.

FRANK: Righto. Yes. Good show, good show.

TERRY: Are you referring to the play, Father – or to my shaking hands?

FRANK: What?

TERRY: Never mind. Come along, Cuthy.

CUTHBERT gives them a little bow. He and TERRY go.

FRANK: Got a spare glass now. Oh well. I'm sure we'll manage it between us. *(He takes two glasses himself.)*

VERA: You might have congratulated him, Frank.

FRANK: Didn't I?

VERA: No. You mumbled something vague, as usual.

FRANK: I'll say something when he comes back. Cheers.

They drink.

What did you think of it then?

VERA: I thought it was excellent. Quite excellent. Sad – but amusing too. You really feel you're right there with them.

FRANK: Mm. Seems to be shaping up at this lark, doesn't he?

VERA: Frank, for goodness' sake –

FRANK: Not sure about him using his war service as the material for a play, though. Doesn't seem right, somehow.

VERA: Why ever not?

FRANK: Not when the war's still on.

VERA: That's all the more reason. It shows what it's really like for the families of bomber pilots. It gives people encouragement.

FRANK: Suppose you have a point.

VERA: Really, Frank, you are impossible. You agree to his trying to make a living in the theatre, and when he gets his plays on in the West End, you seem to begrudge it. You should be pleased for him.

FRANK: I am. I am.

VERA: Then tell him.

FRANK: He doesn't need me to tell him. He doesn't need my opinion.

VERA: He wants your opinion above all else! It's you he most wants to impress. Don't you see that?

FRANK: Can't say that I do.

VERA sighs with impatience.

VERA: Oh, you men…

FRANK starts the second glass of champagne.

FRANK: Steady sort of chap, that Cuthbert.

VERA: Yes. He's a good friend to Terence.

FRANK: Needs all the friends he can get in this line of business.

They become aware of someone lurking in the shadows by the entrance. It is KENNETH MORGAN. He is a young man of small stature and boyish good looks, in his early 20s. He is wearing a dinner jacket and is in an agitated state. The sound of the audience leaving recedes.

VERA: Hello. Can we help you?

KENNETH: *(Light English voice.)* I was looking for Terry.

VERA: He's not here, I'm afraid.

FRANK: He's gone to shake a few hands with people.

VERA: Are you a friend of his?

KENNETH: Yes. I…we've met. Kenneth. Kenneth Morgan. I was in Terry's last play.

VERA: *(Searching her memory.)* Ah, yes…

KENNETH: We met at the first night party. You're his parents, aren't you?

VERA: We are indeed. How do you do?

KENNETH: How do you do.

He nervously shakes their hands.

I played Paul. It didn't do very well. The play. Unlike his first one. I was in the film of that.

VERA: Oh, really? That's nice.

KENNETH: Yes. I got an award in fact. Best Performance by a Newcomer.

VERA: Congratulations.

KENNETH: Well, it's a while ago now…

FRANK: Shall we give him a message for you?

KENNETH: I've got to see him.

VERA: Mr Morgan, I'm afraid we don't arrange our son's social activities. Perhaps you'd like to come back a little later. Or see him at the party.

KENNETH: I didn't think there was going to be a party.

CUTHBERT hurries in, tries to divert KENNETH away from them.

CUTHBERT: Kenneth, what are you doing in here?

KENNETH: I want to talk to Terry.

CUTHBERT: Terry's with the Air Chief Marshal. Come along, I'll get you a drink.

VERA: Cuthbert, I think we'll be on our way now. Please give Terence our love. I'm sure he's very busy. We'll speak to him tomorrow.

CUTHBERT: Yes, all right, Mrs R. Thank you. I'll tell him.

VERA: Come along, Frank.

FRANK polishes off the champagne.

FRANK: Righto. 'Night, Cuthbert.

CUTHBERT: Good night, Major.

FRANK: *(As they go.)* Odd sort of fellow. Who was that chap?

VERA: *(Offstage.)* Don't you listen to anything anyone says…?

They are gone. CUTHBERT rounds on KENNETH.

CUTHBERT: What on earth do you think you're doing, Kenneth? You can't just go introducing yourself like that –

KENNETH: Why? They're not royalty, are they?

CUTHBERT: No, but you know Terry's feelings on the matter.

KENNETH: What about my feelings?

CUTHBERT: Look, I do sympathise. Terry isn't exactly the –

KENNETH: Sympathise? You don't sympathise. You hate me.

CUTHBERT: Not at all –

KENNETH: You all hate me.

CUTHBERT: Who? Who hates you?

KENNETH: All of you. All Terry's friends and hangers-on, and busybodies who keep interfering in his life all the time. Why can't you leave him alone? Why can't you let him lead his own life the way he really wants to?

CUTHBERT: And that's with you, is it?

KENNETH: Yes! With me! As equal partners.

CUTHBERT: Well, now you're just being unreasonable.

KENNETH: Why? What's so unreasonable about being with the person you love?

CUTHBERT: I'm going to get cross now, Kenneth –

KENNETH: Oh, are you? Ooh.

CUTHBERT: You don't love Terry. Not truly –

KENNETH: How dare you! How dare you tell me what I feel or don't feel!

CUTHBERT: You, like all the others, are flattered by his attentions because he's glamorous and in the public eye. You kid yourselves you're in love because that way it justifies your using him mercilessly for your own ends.

KENNETH: That is absolutely ridic–

CUTHBERT: No, it's not! What you fail to understand, Ken, is that older and wiser people than you see straight through you. Where would you be without Terry? Nowhere.

KENNETH: Terry loves me, and I –

CUTHBERT: Yes, well, that I do agree with. Terry does love you, God help him. He always seems to fall for whining little pretty-boys who think the world owes them a living. What is it with you people, you – the good-looking ones of this world – why do you think you're so special? Do you ever spare a thought for the rest of us? Ever? No, you just sneer and dismiss us because you think we're simply not in your league – not worthy of your consideration!

TERRY enters.

TERRY: What *have* I stumbled upon here? Dearie me.

CUTHBERT: Oh, Terry, I – sorry, I was just telling Kenneth that he can't – he was here, with your mother and father –

TERRY: What!

CUTHBERT: Don't worry – they've gone. All is well.

KENNETH: Terry, I need to talk to you!

TERRY: I've never had to shake so many military hands in my life. Such fearsome grasps they have. My hand is quite limp.

KENNETH: Terry, I can't put up with it any longer!

TERRY: *(Finally paying attention to him.)* What is that, Kenny love?

KENNETH: You. The way you treat me. The whole – thing – between us.

TERRY: Oh, please, not another bout of your hysterics. I'm really not up to it tonight.

KENNETH: I'm not being hysterical. I'm just sick and tired of being treated like a nobody.

TERRY: You know I'm devoted to you.

KENNETH: And how do you show it? You stick me halfway back in the circle! Everyone else – everyone who counts – is in the front stalls! You deliberately keep me away from anyone who matters, as if you're ashamed of me! As if I'm some dirty little secret. No one must know about little Kenny, oh no, that would never do.

TERRY: What do you want, Kenneth?

KENNETH: I want to live with you, properly.

TERRY: No, dear, you want to live with me *im*properly, but you can't. My career wouldn't survive, my mother would have a heart attack, and we'd both be arrested. So, please, be a love, and don't –

KENNETH: I mean it, Terry. I'm giving you a choice.

TERRY: Are you now?

TERRY takes a cigarette out of his cigarette case.

CUTHBERT: Shall I go?

TERRY: No. Stay, Cuthy. If you would.

TERRY lights his cigarette.

You are going to tell me that you have an alternative offer, aren't you?

KENNETH: Yes.

TERRY: That doesn't surprise me. You've been ridiculously unfaithful while I've been posted to Coastal Command.

KENNETH: You won't let me be with you!

TERRY: Does your need to be with someone, constantly, override all your other needs?

KENNETH: Yes. It does.

TERRY: Kenny, I keep you in champagne, suits, and you have every possible accoutrement. Watches, cigarette cases, cash – you name it, I have given it to you. Why do you think I do this?

KENNETH: Because you want to keep me on a leash, like a puppydog.

TERRY: Aha. I sniff the influence of another person here. That is not you talking, my love, that is another person putting words into your pretty little mouth, along with everything else he puts there.

KENNETH: No, it's what I think!

TERRY: Then you are an ungrateful brat.

KENNETH: *(His face twisting with sudden rage.)* You can't talk to me like that!

TERRY: Why ever not? It could easily be the truth.

KENNETH: But it isn't the truth! I'm not a brat, and I'm not ungrateful! And I'm not your puppydog either, to be allowed out of my kennel when you say so – when there are no important people, or celebrities, or journalists around!

TERRY: So tell me. What is the choice you are offering me?

KENNETH: Let me move in with you. Permanently.

TERRY: Or?

KENNETH: Or I go and live with someone else.

TERRY: And that someone being?

KENNETH: It doesn't matter.

TERRY: No, you're quite right. It doesn't matter in the least who it is. But I assume it's someone who will not be able to keep you in the manner to which you have so readily become accustomed. Where, may I ask, would you be living if you took this course?

KENNETH: It doesn't *matter.*

TERRY: Oh, but I think it does. To you.

KENNETH: All right. Marylebone.

TERRY: The scruffy end, I imagine. Oh, Kenny, why must you try me like this? Why can't you accept me as I am – as I have to be?

KENNETH: Because it's not enough!

Pause. TERRY carefully puts out his cigarette, apparently completely in control of myself, then suddenly grasps KENNETH to him in a desperate embrace.

TERRY: You are my perfect boy…. Don't do it, Kenny, don't leave me, please…I couldn't bear it. I simply couldn't bear it!

Still clutching KENNETH to him, he erupts into a few heaving sobs. CUTHBERT looks away, bewildered and embarrassed, and perhaps even a little hurt.

Have your other affairs if you must, but don't abandon me…

KENNETH: *(Calmly.)* But can I move in with you, for good?

TERRY clutches him even closer, but says nothing. KENNETH slowly extricates himself.

I think I have my answer. And you have yours.

He moves away. Looks at CUTHBERT, then back at TERRY.

You won't see me again.

He leaves. TERRY slumps into a chair, holds out his hand. CUTHBERT takes it, wraps it in his own.

Spot on OLDER TERRY.

OLDER TERRY: It nearly destroyed me when Kenneth left me. I allowed myself to be too wrapped up in him, his youth, his…looks. Dear God, one is such a slave to it all. But there is also the experience of, once again, finding oneself being seduced by…I won't say a man old enough to be my father – that would be far too Freudian, as well as completely inaccurate – but an older man, certainly, and a man, as they say, of the world. Chips Channon seduced me with a gold cigarette box from Cartier, an Aubusson carpet and a drawing by Augustus John. One can't resist seduction when it comes wrapped in such style. We had a perfect gentlemen's agreement. No ties, no jealousies, just the pleasures of the flesh and a lot of mutual flattery. He had a libido the equal of my own.

More importantly, he believed in me. In my ability to be more than a mere *boulevardier*, and the author of light, youthful comedies. He gave me the courage to write *The Winslow Boy* and *The Browning Version*. If ever I had to justify my choice of career before a heavenly jury – and this is as close to a heavenly jury as I shall probably ever get – I would want *The Browning Version* to be the play to represent me.

Lights fade on OLDER TERRY.

Music.

SCENE FIVE. 1947.

TERRY's set of chambers in Albany, Mayfair. Late evening.

YOUNGER TERRY is holding court with CUTHBERT and FREDDIE in attendance. FREDDIE is a middle-aged man of supreme self-confidence and self-consciousness; he is imposing rather than handsome, a very precise and snappy dresser, unlike CUTHBERT who, in his ordinary lounge suit, has a dowdy, somewhat rumpled, appearance. FREDDIE is able, in this company, to give full rein to his theatrical mannerisms and waspish wit.

TERRY and FREDDIE are drinking whisky, while CUTHBERT nurses an empty glass.

TERRY: … Finally, *finally*, I hear that Gielgud's going to be in New York at the same time as me, so I ring him up and ask if we can meet. *(Imitating.)* 'Oh dear boy, that would be divine'.

FREDDIE: Oh, that's so like him, it really is.

TERRY: We meet in Central Park. Probably because JG thinks he can be more evasive out in the open air. Anyway, I say 'Johnny darling, have you thought about Crocker-Harris?' And he says, 'My dear, I've thought of little else.'

FREDDIE shrieks with laughter at TERRY's impersonation and slaps his knees in delight.

KENNETH MORGAN appears, casually dressed, very much at home. FREDDIE waves his whisky tumbler in the direction of KENNETH, who reluctantly obliges and tops up FREDDIE's glass. CUTHBERT declines with a shake of the head. TERRY automatically holds out his glass for a top up as he recommences his story.

Now, you have to remember that at least a year, if not eighteen months previously, he has said he would 'adore' to play my emotionally restrained schoolmaster in *The Browning Version.* He heaped such lavish praise on it that I thought he'd bite my hand off if I didn't inscribe his name on the script there and then. Anyway, JG dithers, and dithers, and then does something else, and then the theatre is no longer available, and then he wants to put it on hold till he's finished some other boring project – which, fool that I am I agree to do. Well, I wrote it for him! He *is* Crocker-Harris. I've wanted him in a play of mine ever since Oxford, and this is my fourth attempt at getting him to commit to a role. Fourth! I was desperately hurt that he turned down the last part I wrote for him –

CUTHBERT: The barrister in *The Winslow Boy* –

TERRY: Just so, Cuthy. And why did he turn it down? Because Sir Robert doesn't appear until Act Two. It's the star part. It has the best build-up for a character and he has the best curtain line since *Hedda Gabler*. But will Gielgud do it? No, he will not. Which is why I am now so utterly determined to get him to commit to *The Browning Version*.

FREDDIE: Ooh, I can't bear this – I know what's coming –

TERRY: Hold your horses, Freddie. We discuss the play, we discuss the part, we discuss designers. There we are like a couple of old schoolgirls from Roedean, chuckling away for all we are worth about the fun of it all, and he says he wants to do it. 'More than anything, dear boy, I want to be in a play by you. You know that. You have a very special talent, Terry,' he says, loftily, to the wide open spaces of Central Park, 'and nothing would give me greater pleasure than to be Crocker-Harris for you.' Well. We're there. Finally. Finally, I've got him.

FREDDIE: No, don't – don't – I can't stand it!

TERRY: And then he looks wistfully into the distance, as if remembering some treasured little moment in a favourite cottage, and he says, almost as an afterthought, 'But, you know, dear boy, I have to be so careful of new plays these days.'

CUTHBERT: *What?*

TERRY: Yes. Those exact words. And I say, 'What do you mean, Johnny?' And he says, 'Audiences have seen me in so much first-rate stuff, Terry – do you really think they'll like me in something second-rate?'

FREDDIE: No! He didn't!

TERRY: Cross my heart, darlings, those were his very words. Foot straight in it. As always. There I am, pen virtually in hand with the ink dripping off the nib, waiting for him to sign – and there's Binkie in London, and Harold in New York, and we're all waiting for the final say-so, and he goes and ditches me with a line like that. Can you believe it! Me, the prettiest playwright in London – his words, not mine. Anyway…that's the story of Johnny G and The Crock. Fated never to meet, or so it seems.

FREDDIE: Well, she's so fucking grand since she gave her Mrs Hamlet. All that posing with a noble profile. Frankly, I'd have my nose done if I had one like hers. I'd be round Harley Street before you could say 'Oh that this too, too solid flesh would melt.' Ooh, that's rather good, actually, isn't it, especially after all the booze I've had tonight… What a clever little girl I am. Another one, please, Kenneth.

KENNETH emerges again and pours drinks for FREDDIE, TERRY and himself. Again CUTHBERT signals no.

CUTHBERT: What do you think of that, then, Kenneth?

KENNETH: I wouldn't mind doing it.

FREDDIE: Well, we know that, ducky.

KENNETH: I meant the play.

FREDDIE: No! Really?

CUTHBERT: You must get it on, Terry. It's a remarkable piece.

TERRY: Supportive as ever…

CUTHBERT: Seriously, I mean it. Your best so far. Crocker-Harris is an extraordinary portrait of a man disintegrating through lack of love. And the scene with the schoolboy Taplow is one of the most moving I have ever read.

KENNETH: Is there a part in it for me, Terry?

TERRY: You are very young and gorgeous, Kenny, and Crocker-Harris is a classics master in his forties.

KENNETH: I didn't mean Crocker-Harris.

TERRY: I don't think even you, in all your youth and gorgeousness, could be my Taplow.

KENNETH: Why not? I can play really young. I can be sixteen if you like.

FREDDIE: That sounds tempting.

CUTHBERT: Freddie…

KENNETH: *(Deadly serious.)* Well, why not? Can I audition for you, Terry? You liked me in *French Without Tears*.

FREDDIE: That was the film version, dear. The camera does all the work. You have to be able to project on stage.

KENNETH: I'm not a complete beginner, you know! How about it, Terry?

FREDDIE: Oh, do fuck off, ducky. Honestly, Terry, I think you've made a big mistake letting young Kenneth back into your life after the way he treated you last time.

KENNETH: That's not fair!

FREDDIE: He only wants you for your employment opportunities.

KENNETH: That isn't true!

FREDDIE: Well, forgive me, dear, but you can barely talk about anything else. And I can't say your career has exactly blossomed in the last few years, has it? Now I may not be the world's greatest psychoanalyst, but I would hazard a guess that your ill luck in your chosen profession is not entirely unrelated to your desperate need to crawl back between Terry's sheets. Once bitten twice 'fuck off, you little sponger' is the way I'd sum it up, Terry.

TERRY: Yes, Freddie. You've always been known to venture an opinion in the most colourful terms. Especially when not asked. All right, let's have an audition.

KENNETH: Oh, thank you! When will it be?

TERRY: I was rather thinking we'd do it now.

TERRY goes to the desk, takes two typescripts from a drawer.

KENNETH: Now?

TERRY: I'll be the Crock and you can be Taplow. Freddie and Cuthbert can be Binkie Beaumont and the money. They can judge your performance.

FREDDIE: This sounds like fun…

KENNETH: Well, I… it's a bit late, isn't it?

TERRY: Start here. I'm the Classics master that nobody likes, who is about to leave the school, and you are one of my pupils.

TERRY takes a small book from his desk.

Here. You'll need this. *(Hands it to him.)* You knock at the door.

KENNETH gathers himself. Clears his throat, knocks on a piece of furniture.

TERRY: *(As Crocker-Harris.)* Come in.

KENNETH 'enters', boyishly.

Yes, Taplow? What is it?

KENNETH: Nothing, sir.

TERRY: What do you mean, nothing?

KENNETH: *(Timidly.)* I just came back to say goodbye, sir.

TERRY: Oh.

KENNETH: I didn't have a chance with the head here. I rather dashed out, I'm afraid. I thought I'd just come back and – wish you luck, sir.

TERRY: Thank you, Taplow. That's good of you.

KENNETH: I – er – thought this might interest you, sir.

TERRY: What is it?

KENNETH: *(Holding it out like an offering.)* It's a verse translation of *The Agamemnon*, sir. The Browning version. It's not much good. I've been reading it in the Chapel gardens.

TERRY takes the book. His eyes meet KENNETH's.

TERRY: Very interesting, Taplow. *(He seems to have a little difficulty in speaking. He clears his throat, and goes on in a gentle, level voice.)* I know the translation, of course. It has its faults, I agree, but I think you will enjoy it more when you get used to the metre he employs.

TERRY hands the book back.

KENNETH: *(Returning it and looking him in the eye.)* It's for you, sir.

TERRY: For me?

KENNETH: Yes, sir. I've written in it.

TERRY opens the fly-leaf and reads what is 'written' there.

TERRY: Did you buy this?

KENNETH: Yes, sir. It was only second-hand.

TERRY: You shouldn't have spent your pocket money this way.

KENNETH: That's all right, sir. It wasn't very much. *(Suddenly appalled.)* The price isn't still inside, is it?

TERRY: *(At length.)* No. Just what you've written. Nothing else.

KENNETH: Good. I'm sorry you've got it already. I thought you probably would have.

TERRY: I haven't got it already. I may have had it once. I can't remember. But I haven't got it now.

KENNETH: That's all right then. *(Pause. Then, suspiciously:)* What's the matter, sir? Have I got the accent wrong on *eumenose*?

TERRY: No. The perispomenon is perfectly correct. *(His hands are shaking. He lowers the book and turns away from KENNETH.)* Taplow, would you be good enough to take that bottle of medicine, which you so kindly brought in, and pour me out one dose in a glass which you will find in the bathroom?

KENNETH: *(Seeing something is wrong.)* Yes, sir.

TERRY: The doses are clearly marked on the bottle. I usually put a little water with it.

KENNETH: Yes, sir.

TERRY has his head in his hands, overcome by an emotion that has taken him by surprise. The others watch, uncertain whether this is in the scene, or is real. Slowly, TERRY pulls himself together.

TERRY: *(As himself again.)* Taplow exits to bathroom. The Crock breaks down and sobs uncontrollably at the inscription written by the boy, a quotation from the play referring to 'a gentle master'. All his emotional sterility suddenly bursts forth at this simple, and completely unexpected, act of kindness. His mask has slipped – or, rather, been wrenched aside.

CUTHBERT: Wonderful, Terry. A wonderful scene. It's bound to be a huge success.

FREDDIE: Bravo, my dear. And a most touching reading.

KENNETH: *(Pleased with himself.)* Thanks. Sight reading isn't usually a strength of mine.

FREDDIE: I was referring to Terry.

KENNETH: Oh.

CUTHBERT: You read it well, Kenny.

KENNETH: Thanks. Most Promising Newcomer, you know.

FREDDIE: Oh, Christ, not that fucking accolade again. I think we've heard quite enough about your youthful promise, dear.

KENNETH: Was it all right, Terry? Was I any good?

TERRY: Go and get into bed and I'll tell you later.

KENNETH looks at him, still hoping for a word of praise.

But you have to be out before morning.

KENNETH: Why?

TERRY: Because I say so.

KENNETH: Yes, but…why, Terry?

TERRY: You know why.

KENNETH: Because you have to work…

TERRY: Yes. And because I fully expect Chips Channon to come round for coffee.

KENNETH: Oh. Does he have to?

TERRY: Have coffee? Probably not, no. He doesn't usually bother. *(A beat.)* Run along then, there's a dear. And say good night to Freddie and Cuthbert.

KENNETH: Good night.

FREDDIE: Don't do anything I wouldn't do.

CUTHBERT: That's not saying much.

FREDDIE: Bitch.

CUTHBERT: Good night, Kenneth.

KENNETH slowly turns and leaves.

TERRY: Don't say anything, Freddie. I know. He hasn't changed. As sulky as ever, but you know how it is…

CUTHBERT: You can't resist.

TERRY: No, indeed.

FREDDIE: Chips is far better for you, Terry. You know that.

CUTHBERT: It has to be said that there's a world of difference between them.

FREDDIE: I should coco! A knight of the realm and man of the world on the one hand – and a struggling little actor on the other. Chalk and the proverbial cheddar.

CUTHBERT: And Chips doesn't want to cling on to you all the time.

FREDDIE: He likes to keep things uncomplicated. Passion at bay.

TERRY: Yes, yes, yes! But he's not a fresh-faced, wide-eyed 20-year-old, is he?

A beat.

CUTHBERT: There is that.

TERRY: So, come along, dears. Beddy-byes.

CUTHBERT: *(Starting to go.)* Will you consider Kenneth for the part, Terry?

TERRY: I think you know the answer to that.

CUTHBERT: But you'll let him believe he might get it?

TERRY: You know the answer to that one too.

FREDDIE: You're such a heartless old tart, Terry. I love it!

TERRY: *(With a sheepish smile.)* It's naughty of me, I know, but I just adore having them in my power. He'll do anything I want. Anything. His desire to please me will be worth a hundred ordinary erections.

FREDDIE laughs and gives TERRY a big hug.

FREDDIE: Night night, you naughty, naughty girl.

CUTHBERT: You shouldn't have taken him back. You'll regret it and so will he.

TERRY: Don't be such an old nanny, Cuthbert. Bugger off home and let a lady take her pleasure while she can.

They go.

Spot on OLDER TERRY.

OLDER TERRY: Cuthbert was quite right, of course. He usually was. But, as usual, I didn't listen. I simply never got into the habit. *The Browning Version* eventually got produced – without John Gielgud – and was, as Cuthbert predicted, a great success. And I don't think Kenneth ever forgave me. He left me for a second time. But no one is ever irreplaceable. Not in the theatre, and not in life. And my poor little Kenneth was replaced by Michael. Dear Christ, I missed him though. He had...something that I needed very badly. Not just looks, and willingness, but he...he knew what I wanted, in every sense. He knew *me*. The artful little shit. And the more he sulked and pouted, the more he treated me with his particular brand of calculated indifference, the more I wanted to hug him, crush him, possess him, like a disobedient, mischievous cherub.

I didn't realise it then, but he was my own lost self coming to haunt me. No wonder he couldn't survive.

Lights down on OLDER TERRY.

Music.

SCENE SIX. 1952.

Little Court, Sunningdale, Berkshire (TERRY's house next to the golf course). Late morning. Perhaps some birdsong outside.

YOUNGER TERRY is in the middle of a telephone conversation. He enters, holding the telephone. CUTHBERT is seated in the room and FREDDIE is idly practising a few putts with a golf club. They are all drinking champagne. There is a large scrapbook of press cuttings open on the floor.

TERRY: ... So I understand, yes. The *Observer* and the *New Statesman* in particular. Terribly gratifying. But, my dear, I wouldn't dream of comparing it to *In Which We Serve...* It was just the luck of the... it was just timing. No box office record stands for ever... Well, it's sweet of you to say so, Noël. I truly appreciate... I've always been envious of you, you know that! No, truly. And Churchill seemed to like it too.

Yes. Private screening. But that's only because he's the... No, no, actually it wasn't my idea. Have to say. I simply came up with the words. So you see – pure hackwork. That's very naughty of you, but... No, I wouldn't. Absolutely not. Noël darling, terribly sweet of you to ring up… You too. Bless you. Yes. Yes. Yes indeed… Soon. Promise.

He puts the receiver down, turns to the others.

That was Noël.

CUTHBERT: You don't say.

FREDDIE: Noël who? *(Cackles with laughter.)* Honestly, get you, dear. There's no need to be quite so unctuous. I mean, she's not exactly God, is she?

TERRY: I couldn't help it. One feels so…well, flattered.

MICHAEL enters, wearing a dressing gown and pyjamas, and looking somewhat dishevelled. He is short in stature, slim, with schoolboy looks, as befits his tender years (early 20s). At first we might mistake him for KENNETH in his general appearance and his ability to be completely at home in TERRY's house.

MICHAEL goes to the drinks table and pours himself a slug of champagne from the open bottle, much to the disapproval of FREDDIE and CUTHBERT. He sees TERRY's open book of press cuttings and idly leafs through it.

FREDDIE: Don't be a silly bitch. She knows *Deep Blue Sea* is miles better than anything she could toss off in a few days, but she can't bring herself to say anything about that, so she saves face by ringing up about your film. *(To MICHAEL.)* How very nice to see you so early in the day, Michael. And thanks so much for pouring *us* a drinkie while you were about it.

MICHAEL: *(Soft American accent.)* I'm not the butler around here.

TERRY: Michael, do the honours, there's a good boy.

MICHAEL: I could call Lockwood if you want.

TERRY: Lockwood's helping prepare lunch. Do be a love.

FREDDIE: I suppose you've invited yourself to lunch as well?

MICHAEL: I have, as a matter of fact.

FREDDIE: Well, there's bold for you. Quite making ourselves at home, aren't we?

MICHAEL begrudgingly pours champagne for them.

No grace or charm, you notice.

CUTHBERT: None.

FREDDIE: Now, Terry, I want to have a word with you about *French Without Tears* –

TERRY: Are you going to be vulgar, Freddie, and talk shop before lunch?

FREDDIE: I just want you to let me do a musical version. It would be an absolute winner, dear, and you know it. And who better to direct it than me? Line your pockets while you can, that's what I say.

TERRY: I know how keen you are, my dear, but after the success of *Deep Blue Sea* it would be a retrograde step.

FREDDIE: *(Stung.)* Retrograde? With me at the helm? I flatter myself, Terry, that I would see to it that it was no such thing. I'm surprised at you, truly I am.

TERRY and MICHAEL exchange glances. CUTHBERT notices this, and looks away.

TERRY: Are you going to change, Midget? *(Dryly.)* You look a little overdressed for lunch.

FREDDIE: We could play pass the parcel with her, and unwrap her layer by layer.

MICHAEL: You know, Terry, I really think we might re-do the décor in this room.

TERRY: Why? Do you not approve?

MICHAEL: A duck egg blue would work better. With white curtains and a cream carpet.

FREDDIE: Hark at her. She's already redesigning the house.

TERRY: Actually, Michael is an interior designer.

FREDDIE: She's not coming anywhere near my interior.

TERRY: I think duck egg blue sounds rather fetching.

MICHAEL: Try me. My fee is very modest.

FREDDIE: Is nothing sacred? She wants paying now. She wants you to set her up in business, that's what this is all about –

TERRY: Of course that's what he wants. Isn't it, Midget?

MICHAEL, suddenly embarrassed, merely smiles.

MICHAEL: I think I'll go and change. Leave you lovely people to talk about me all you want.

He goes, leaving his champagne glass.

CUTHBERT: Bullseye there, I think, Freddie.

FREDDIE: I've seen some naked ambition in my time, Terry, but that takes the Victoria fucking sponge. It honestly does. She's organising you like a mincing little majorette. You've only known her for five minutes.

TERRY: Very amusing, Freddie, dear, but you see the fact is I'm completely smitten.

CUTHBERT: You usually are.

FREDDIE: *(To TERRY.)* You like them short and sweet, with nice schoolboy faces, don't you, dear? It's always the same. Takes you back to your golden years at Harrow – all that pent-up testosterone in the dorm.

TERRY: Freddie, you are becoming quite masturbatory. Please desist.

CUTHBERT: Seriously, Terry, I would urge caution as far as young Michael is concerned. He's made no secret of the fact that he wants to be looked after, in considerable style, by somebody famous. He even had Benjamin Britten chasing after him for a while.

TERRY: That was a *very* lucky escape.

FREDDIE shrieks with laughter.

CUTHBERT: He's clearly on the make, and he doesn't care how he gets there.

TERRY: Do you find it unseemly, Cuthy?

CUTHBERT: It's so flagrant. So utterly transparent it's almost indecent.

FREDDIE: Grubby little chancer, Terry, that's the truth of it. She'd suck off Frankenstein's monster for a gin and tonic.

TERRY: Thank you for that delightful analogy, Freddie.

FREDDIE: And as for that phoney American accent – lends no glamour at all. She'd be better off pretending to be Hungarian.

TERRY: We all know about your penchant for Eastern Europeans, Freddie. So very democratic of you.

FREDDIE: I love it when they speak no English. Makes it so much more exciting.

CUTHBERT: Is he going to be here this evening when your guests arrive?

TERRY: Absolutely not. Mother is coming.

A beat.

FREDDIE: Does your mama still know nothing of the real you, Terry?

TERRY: Nothing. And it will remain that way. To her I am a decent, upstanding, thoroughly respectable, law-abiding chap, of whom she can be proud in the best possible motherly way. In fact her pride in me is what keeps her going, even if I say so myself. I couldn't conceive of dragging her through all the unpleasantness that would ensue if she knew the truth.

CUTHBERT: Quite right. It would be the death of her.

TERRY: Possibly even literally, Cuthy, yes.

FREDDIE: I think she might be a lot cannier than you realise.

TERRY: My dear Freddie, one thing my mother is *not* is canny.

FREDDIE: I think she might be playing up to the image of yourself that you choose to present to the world. She doesn't want to upset you.

TERRY: Complete rot.

FREDDIE: If you say so.

CUTHBERT: How is the redoubtable Mrs R?

TERRY: As well as can be expected, as the doctors say. She took the news about my father very badly, I'm afraid.

CUTHBERT: Unlike you.

TERRY: Not at all. I was very upset. Still am. As I also am about my brother Brian.

FREDDIE gives an inquiring look.

He's been diagnosed with cancer of the lung.

FREDDIE: Oh my goodness.

CUTHBERT: Very sad. Very very sad.

TERRY: I feel rather guilty about poor Brian.

FREDDIE: Why? It's not your –

TERRY: I've been a very poor brother.

CUTHBERT: *(Gently.)* Not true…

TERRY: Watching him struggle all those years trying to qualify as a solicitor while I'm lording it in the West End. Barely gave him a thought, let alone a word of encouragement. Leaves a nasty taste in the mouth. *(Before FREDDIE can say anything.)* No innuendo, please, Freddie.

FREDDIE: I shan't say a word.

Small silence. CUTHBERT decides to try and break it.

CUTHBERT: I met an interesting chap at a literary lunch the other day. Used to write for a magazine called *Startling Stories…*

MICHAEL re-enters, now dressed in sweater, open-necked shirt and slacks. No-one pays any attention to CUTHBERT's remark.

FREDDIE: Oh hello. The rent-boy is back.

MICHAEL: You go out of your way to be offensive, don't you?

FREDDIE: Not at all. It requires no deviation whatsoever. Where are you from, Michael?

MICHAEL: *(Collecting his glass from where he left it.)* Notting Hill.

FREDDIE: I mean originally.

MICHAEL: Chelsea.

FREDDIE: There you are! Not American at all!

MICHAEL: I was brought up in Connecticut from the age of six. I moved there from London when my mother died. I am half-English, but my accent, believe it or not, is entirely genuine.

CUTHBERT: *(Quietly)* Touché, I think.

FREDDIE: A word of warning, Michael. Don't presume too far, just because you have a pretty face.

TERRY: Oh do leave the boy alone! I'm fed up with hearing how he's simply *using* me. You all use me.

FREDDIE: *Do* we?

TERRY: Yes, you do! I know perfectly well that you tell stories against me to all your other friends just to get a cheap laugh. You'd do anything, say anything, just to get a laugh – even if it means betraying confidences.

FREDDIE gapes at him.

FREDDIE: I, Terry?

TERRY: Yes, you, Freddie. You hang off my coat-tails because I am the man of the moment and you are desperate to use your friendship with me as a mark of your own importance. Christ knows why I put up with you. And as for you, Cuthy, you use your loyalty to me as a mask for your own inadequacy. You both use me shamelessly. It's the price I have to pay to have a few friendly faces around me.

MICHAEL: Well said, Terry.

A beat.

FREDDIE: Well, that's us well and truly told, isn't it? Slapped wrists all round.

CUTHBERT: *(Hurt.)* I'm sorry, Terry. I had no idea you felt that way.

MICHAEL decides to drive home this advantage.

MICHAEL: And while we're on the subject, I'll thank you not to refer to me as a rent-boy.

FREDDIE: It's what you are. Except you seem to be rented by the week rather than the hour.

MICHAEL: That's enough, do you hear! I won't put up with this! I won't! I'm here because Terry wants me to be here! It's as simple as that. And I will not be insulted by a jealous old queen like you!

TERRY: Michael, Michael…

FREDDIE: And what, precisely, gives you the right to talk to us like that, young man? What exactly have you done in life to earn the right to scream and shout and lay down the law? Who, precisely, are you, might one ask?

MICHAEL: Who are *you*, come to that?

FREDDIE: My dear child, I am a theatre director of some repute, as anyone who knows will tell you. I have been responsible for six major productions in the West End and on tour, starring some of the most illustrious fucking names in British theatre. I have also appeared in three others –

TERRY: I don't think we need a recitation of your CV, Freddie.

FREDDIE: In other words – in my chosen profession I am what you might call Somebody. And Mr Worsley here is a journalist, critic and author of no small renown. I think a little respect is due from a mid-Atlantic nobody who is trying to worm his way into the top drawer of London society without the slightest sense of his own good fortune, and who is quite prepared to stick his mid-Atlantic cock anywhere that gains him material advantage –

MICHAEL: You can't lecture me! You have no right! I don't care how many shows you've been in, or directed – I'm just as good as you are!

FREDDIE: And that is quite the most fatuous remark you have made to date.

MICHAEL: Oh yes, go on, insult me! You're just jealous because I wouldn't look twice at you –

TERRY: Enough! Let's call a halt, shall we?

MICHAEL: I can see now why Kenneth Morgan was driven to suicide if this was what he had to put up with!

CUTHBERT: I beg your pardon?

FREDDIE: *What* did you say?

A deadly silence.

TERRY: What do you know about Kenneth Morgan?

MICHAEL: *(Unstoppable now)* I know he committed suicide by gassing himself, and that's what gave you the idea for *The Deep Blue Sea.*

TERRY: Who did you hear that from?

MICHAEL: I don't know! It doesn't matter! I heard it! And it's true, isn't it?

Pause. FREDDIE and CUTHBERT exchange looks, and cast worried glances at TERRY.

TERRY: I advise you, Michael, that if you value your friendship with me you will not bandy around such wild statements. In fact, I expressly forbid you to mention it again. Do you understand?

MICHAEL's face begins to crumple, like a small child about to burst into tears.

MICHAEL: Why is everyone getting at me today?

TERRY: Because, my dear Michael, I am not prepared to have a lover who talks behind my back and blabs his mouth off inadvisedly. These things can be very dangerous. They can have very serious repercussions. We all live under constant threat of exposure.

MICHAEL: Don't send me away, Terry. Please. Don't send me away.

FREDDIE: I have a feeling you may just have failed your final audition, Michael.

TERRY: Freddie – shut up!

FREDDIE: *(Genuinely crestfallen for once.)* Sorry.

CUTHBERT: Michael, I will just say this. Kenneth Morgan was an unhappy boy who desperately wanted to be part of Terry's life – no, Terry, I think this needs to be said – but he didn't understand the rules. His death had nothing directly to do with Terry, or us, or any of our friends, but, of course, Terry suffered terrible feelings of guilt – as he is suffering now over his brother – feelings which are, to some extent, explored in *The Deep Blue Sea*. That is what happens when you are a writer. You draw on your own experience. You transform your experience, through your imagination, into art, and that art then contains a truth that is recognisable by others – but it is by no means to be confused with being a mere representation of the original experience. It is far, far subtler and more complex than that. So please do not think, for one single solitary moment, that Terry in any way caused a young man's death and then exploited it.

MICHAEL: I...don't.

CUTHBERT: Good. Because some who are envious of Terry's success are quite prepared to believe such vicious rumours.

And Terry's reputation must be safeguarded. We all look after each other in our different ways. That's how it works. *(With a glance at TERRY.)* Even if at times we appear unkind to each other.

FREDDIE: Well said, Cuthy.

TERRY: Most eloquent, my dear. And rather touching. *(He pats him affectionately on the shoulder.)* Now, lunch, I think. You two go on. Ask Lockwood to bring some more champagne.

FREDDIE: Ooh, goody! Come on, Cuthy, let's go and drink ourselves silly…

CUTHBERT: You ought to do something about the Lockwoods, Terry. They steal from you remorselessly.

TERRY: Do they?

FREDDIE: Spend most of the housekeeping money on themselves. You're the only one who doesn't notice.

FREDDIE and CUTHBERT exit.

TERRY looks at MICHAEL, who still appears sorry for himself.

TERRY: *(Gently.)* Come here.

MICHAEL crosses to him.

Are we friends again, my little Midget?

MICHAEL: That's not very nice, calling me a midget.

TERRY: I'm calling you *my* little Midget. There's a world of difference.

MICHAEL: OK…

TERRY: You mustn't mind Freddie and Cuthbert. They are very protective of me.

MICHAEL: They are just so…hostile.

TERRY: It's a hostility tinged with envy.

MICHAEL: Envy? Of who?

TERRY: Of *whom*.

MICHAEL: All right, of whom?

TERRY: Of me, having you. Now, how much money did you lose last night? All of it?

MICHAEL: If you're going to lose, lose in style.

TERRY: *(Laughs.)* I'll take you to a real casino one day. The Hôtel Martinez in Cannes. *There's* a place to lose money in style.

MICHAEL: I'd adore that.

TERRY kisses his forehead.

TERRY: Come along. A little lunch with my two henchmen then it's back to Notting Hill with you.

MICHAEL: Must I?

TERRY: Those are the rules. I have people coming.

MICHAEL: And will I always have to be hidden away like an embarrassing relative? Is that how you do things?

TERRY: My dear Midget, I am one of London's Most Eligible Bachelors. One has to play the part.

MICHAEL: And if I were to throw myself off your balcony – would that spoil your image?

TERRY: Don't start being cantankerous, or you'll make me cross.

MICHAEL: I think being cantankerous is the only way to deal with you, Terry.

TERRY: Then you misjudge me.

MICHAEL holds TERRY's gaze.

And I advise you *not* to misjudge me.

Pause.

MICHAEL: It's true about Mr and Mrs Lockwood. They're robbing you blind. Even I have noticed.

TERRY: I'm a soft touch, I admit. Just can't face confronting them about it.

MICHAEL: Confrontation is not your strong point, is it?

Pause. He touches TERRY's cheek.

I'll do it for you. They'll be gone within a week.

TERRY clasps MICHAEL to him.

Lights up on OLDER TERRY, watching them.

OLDER TERRY: There I am. At the height of my career. In all my weakness and all my strength. And look at me now. Christ, what have I become?

Blackout.

Interval.

Act Two

SCENE ONE. 1958.

Globe Theatre, London. An ante-room to a private box. Evening. Music intro, then the low sound of interval conversation from the auditorium.

VERA and TERRY are standing in silence. TERRY is in evening dress, and looks tired and less youthful. VERA is now an elderly rather than middle-aged lady, but still sprightly and elegantly dressed in an evening gown.

TERRY: *(Eventually.)* They're hating it, aren't they?

VERA: Not at all, dear. The applause was substantial.

TERRY: I'd hardly call it that.

VERA: It wasn't up to the standards of *The Winslow Boy*, certainly, but that was exceptional. Nothing could ever equal that.

A quick look from TERRY.

For the interval applause, I mean. They cheered every curtain. Such a night that was.

VERA sits. TERRY follows suit.

I'm sure this one will be a success, dear. I always trust my lucky champagne cork. *(Produces it from her evening bag.)* See? I still have it.

TERRY: Of course you have. And it's very sweet of you.

VERA: *(Putting the cork away again.)* Are you all right? You seem a little out of sorts.

TERRY gives her a wan smile.

They'll come round in the second act. You'll see.

TERRY: Would you care for a drink?

VERA: No, thank you, dear. But you have one.

TERRY: I will shortly.

VERA: Are you giving a first-night party?

TERRY: *(Unenthusiastic.)* Yes.

VERA: That's grand. Who's going?

TERRY: Rex and Kay. Johnny Gielgud. Cuthbert. Jean Dawnay. The usual crowd.

VERA: And Margaret Leighton?

TERRY: Yes, of course. Obviously the cast are all going.

VERA looks away, a little hurt at his tone.

VERA: All right, dear…

TERRY: Sorry. Didn't mean to snap. Yes, Maggie and all the cast are coming. Plus Hugh Beaumont, the producer, and various others.

VERA: Isn't he the one they call Binkie?

TERRY: *(Surprised that she knows this.)* I believe so, yes.

VERA: What an odd nickname! Binkie… *(Gives a little laugh.)*

TERRY: You know theatre people. Have their little ways. Idiosyncrasies. Anyway, I doubt it'll be much of a celebration.

VERA: Have you fallen out with Margaret?

TERRY: No. Why?

VERA: I think you'd make a splendid couple. She's such a beauty. And you're so handsome, and debonair.

TERRY: Not that again, Mother…

VERA: You need to settle down, dear, or you'll be a dreadful dyed-in-the-wool bachelor for ever.

TERRY: Is that so terrible?

VERA: It would just be a pity. You've got so much to offer, Terence. I don't want to see you wasting your life away.

TERRY: Wasting it? Mother, really…

VERA: And you do like Margaret Leighton, I know you do.

TERRY: Yes. I do. She is a very glamorous, delightful lady, and I'm very fond of her.

VERA: Told you so!

TERRY: But being so glamorous and delightful she has many admirers. And I like to surround myself with plenty of friends rather than commit to one person who would tire of me very quickly. And I of them.

VERA: You don't do yourself justice. I'm sure she'd have you like a shot if you asked her.

TERRY: This is a pointless conversation.

VERA: And there's always Jean Dawnay. She's very attractive – well, as you'd expect from a Dior model. Always in all the magazines.

TERRY: Yes, Mother. Jean is beautiful and charming, and a wonderful hostess.

VERA: What more do you want?

TERRY: Indeed. I'm spoilt for choice.

VERA: You know what someone told me the other day – a fellow-resident at the hotel? That you were 'no ladies' man'. Well, I thought that would be rather a good thing – not to be chasing after women all the time like your father – but she said it with such a sneer, as if she were quite scoring a point against me. Dreadful woman. She kept making reference to people like Cecil Beaton and – who did Margaret's costumes in this?

TERRY: Norman Hartnell.

VERA: Yes. That's the one. She made some really quite offensive remarks. I had to ring your secretary.

TERRY: *(Alarmed.)* You had to do what?

VERA: Nice girl. Very well-spoken.

TERRY: Mother, what did you ring Mary *for*?

VERA: To ask what that ghastly woman Mrs Rillington-Smith was talking about. Such a tongue she has on her. Always wagging away about someone or other. You know, I do believe she can be quite malicious when she turns her mind to it. Just because her husband left most of his money to his daughter in America she thinks she has a right to be unpleasant about people.

TERRY: What did Mary say?

VERA: Oh, she quite put my mind at rest. Said that she clearly meant that you were dedicated to your career and nothing else. And you are, dear. You work extremely hard. You always have.

TERRY: *(Relieved.)* I see.

VERA: And writing plays and films is not so very far removed from designing costumes and hats and things, is it? Well, I know they're very different, but they're both artistic pursuits, aren't they? You know what I mean! And artistic people have to work very hard because they never know if the next design, or play, or whatever, is going to be popular. It's not like working in a bank or somewhere like that.

TERRY: *(Amused now.)* No, Mother, it's nothing like working in a bank.

VERA: You do like to throw lots of parties, though. That's one area in which I do think you could be a bit more circumspect. A little less extravagant.

TERRY: I'll bet my parties aren't a patch on yours in Berlin and Constantinople and wherever else –

VERA: Those were different. They were part of the job, and your father and I weren't footing the bill. Mind you, he was every bit as bad as you in other ways – spent money like water without a thought for tomorrow.

TERRY: Mother, is this a lecture? Because if so, could we please postpone it till after the performance?

VERA: I wish you'd cared for your father a little more.

TERRY holds his tongue, turns away.

A son should try to be fond of both his parents, not just one. Don't misunderstand me, Terry darling, I am tremendously appreciative of all that you've done for me, but –

TERRY: *(Unable to remain silent any longer.)* I am not prepared to discuss this! You know my feelings on the subject. He took you for a fool and that was unforgivable.

VERA is taken aback. Pause. Then a discreet cough from CUTHBERT, who has appeared in the doorway.

CUTHBERT: The curtain is about to go up again.

TERRY gathers himself.

TERRY: Thank you, Cuthy.

VERA: Try not to have unkindness in your heart, Terence. You are a dear, dear boy, but you don't understand everyth–

TERRY: Mother. Please. *(She is silenced.)* Cuthbert, would you be so kind as to see Mother to her seat?

CUTHBERT: It would be a pleasure. Aren't you going to join us?

TERRY: I think not.

CUTHBERT: The mood is very positive downstairs. Very positive.

The interval bell rings.

TERRY: It's kind of you to say so, Cuthy, but there is no denying that the public's tastes have changed. I have no desire to hear them baying for my blood. I shall go to the bar.

CUTHBERT: I'd have thought this was a pleasant change from all that dreary stuff at the Royal Court. Anyway, it'll all blow over. People will soon tire of looking at kitchen sinks and ironing boards as a means of entertainment.

TERRY: I wouldn't count on it. Those boringly earnest young men may have plenty to say, but they have little style and no wit. And I fear that this audience would rather be at one of their stupendously uninspired little dramas. Excuse me.

TERRY exits.

CUTHBERT looks at VERA, smiles.

VERA: I do wonder sometimes if Terence doesn't put too much of himself into his work.

CUTHBERT: I think you're undoubtedly right.

VERA: I do so want him to be happy. Generally, in life, I mean. I know I nag him about marriage, but it's only because I want him to think about that side of things. Even if it's only to decide that he really can't face it at all. I often wonder, you know, if Frank and I have been a bad influence on him. With our marital relationship. You understand, Cuthbert.

CUTHBERT: I do. And I'm sure you have no cause for concern there.

VERA: Thank you. It's kind of you to say so. *(A beat.)* Will it affect him badly if this play gets poor reviews?

CUTHBERT: He's had less than flattering reviews before.

VERA: But it's not a good time for him now, is it?

CUTHBERT: No, indeed. He is somewhat…below par.

The interval bell rings.

VERA: Well, a mother must do what she can. She must always be there, come what may.

CUTHBERT: An admirable thought, Mrs R. An admirable thought. And the same applies to a long-standing friend. *(He proffers his arm.)* Shall we?

VERA: *(As they go.)* Personally, I can't wait to see what happens in the second act. And I'm sure Margaret Leighton will have another splendid gown…

They are gone.

Spot on OLDER TERRY.

OLDER TERRY: 'Mr Rattigan is out of form.' So said *The Daily Telegraph*. 'A shoddy, novelettish romance' said some other paper. And Kenneth Tynan thought the star of the show was Norman Hartnell. He couldn't see much real acting going on at all. So much for my play *Variation on a Theme*. The reviews were some of the worst of my career. I started to become old that night. The mask began to crack.

And to add insult to injury, a young girl from Manchester who saw it on tour decided she could do much better, and wrote a play which opened at Stratford East three weeks after mine opened in the West End. It was called *A Taste of Honey*. To me it was a smack in the face.

He gives a start, suddenly remembering something.

But I'm getting ahead of myself. I'm forgetting Brian. My poor dear Brian.

Lights lower on OLDER TERRY. He remains as an observer.

Music.

SCENE TWO. 1952.

Little Court, Sunningdale. Night.

YOUNGER TERRY is alone, drinking brandy. He has writing paper and a pen in front of him. He is in sombre mood.

TERRY: Dear Brian, it's rather late at night to write letters – 2.15am, but I can't go to bed without getting this effusion off my chest. It's been my profession all my life to use words dishonestly, and now I need them to record, rather than induce, an emotion most honestly and deeply felt, they seem to be taking their revenge on me. I can't really blame them, I suppose. They've been wickedly exploited for the vilest of motives – mere cash.

So I think the best thing is just not to try and find the beastly things at all, but merely to tell you this simple truth – that if ever, and whenever, my time comes to receive news as grave as the news you have received, I can only hope and pray I receive it as well as you have. But I deeply doubt it. Don't use this against me when you get well. But at this moment of trouble and anxiety I thought you should know how much your courage, resignation and unselfishness have helped those who care for you.

Lights up further on OLDER TERRY.

OLDER TERRY: It was the first time I remember letting my guard down. Like Crocker-Harris and *The Browning Version.* My brother's illness touched a chord that had not been touched for a very long time.

TERRY: *(Still addressing his brother.)* Sorry to be embarrassing, but I couldn't avoid it. Some things have to be said.

OLDER TERRY: Oh yes. Sometimes the words must emerge. Escape their confinement.

Lights fade on OLDER TERRY.

TERRY: Do you remember those early years? Cooped up with Grandmother. Two over-dressed little boys being kept in order in case they dared to ask where the hell their parents had gone. What happened to us? Was it when you went away to school? We grew apart so easily, after all those years with nothing but each other. Oh, Brian. I'm so sorry for you now. I'm so sorry to have been so useless to you. *(Returning to his letter)* My love and every possible good wish. Terry.

Christ, he's going to die. At 45. Christ.

He pauses. Drinks. Picks up his pen, but then sets it down again.

MICHAEL enters.

MICHAEL: Terry? Are you OK?

No response.

I think you should stop working now. It's late. It's time to go to bed. I can stay if you like.

A beat.

Would you like me to stay?

A beat.

Let me put you to bed then.

Slowly, wearily, TERRY looks up at him.

Perhaps you were dreaming. Were you? Were you asleep and having a bad dream?

TERRY: I wasn't asleep.

MICHAEL: You mustn't fret over your father.

TERRY: Hm?

MICHAEL: Bereaved people always feel a kind of guilt. You must try not to. You have no cause to feel guilt.

TERRY: What are you talking about?

MICHAEL: Your father. Was not an easy man, I know.

TERRY: Oh, really?

MICHAEL: Yes. You've told me as much. And I know he meant a lot to you, nevertheless.

TERRY: You seem to know a lot about me for someone I've only known for five minutes.

MICHAEL: *(Laughs.)* Five minutes! It feels like half a lifetime to me.

TERRY: Are you for real, Michael? Are you? Or are you just a fabrication?

MICHAEL: I don't know what you mean.

TERRY: Are you trying to fashion yourself into the creature you think I want?

MICHAEL: That sounds a little weird.

TERRY: Yes, doesn't it?

Pause.

MICHAEL: I could stay with you tonight, Terry. If you need me. And I think you do.

MICHAEL goes to TERRY and touches him. He takes TERRY's hand and places it on his crotch.

That's what you want, isn't it?

TERRY snatches his hand away.

TERRY: Little Mister Cocksure. So certain of yourself. It doesn't always come down to sex, Michael. There are other things that perhaps you don't understand – perhaps you never will understand –

MICHAEL: Oh well, if you're going to fly off the fucking handle! I'm only trying to be nice! Anyway, you *do* normally want that. Don't deny it!

TERRY: So temperamental. I'm tired, Michael…

MICHAEL: Well, I'll just go and slit my wrists then. See how you like that!

TERRY: Not now. Not that again.

MICHAEL: I'm boring you, am I?

TERRY: No…

MICHAEL: I'll go and get the kitchen knife! I'm going to do it, Terry! If you don't want me – if you'd rather be here on your own, and ramble on to yourself all night, well, fine, you do that. I needn't be here. I've tried to do it before, you know!

TERRY: Michael, Michael, calm down –

MICHAEL: I have almost done it!

TERRY: I'm sure.

MICHAEL: So. Don't make me try again.

TERRY: I'll try not to.

Pause. MICHAEL is still worked up.

MICHAEL: I won't be ignored, Terry. That's the issue. I'd rather die than be ignored.

TERRY: I know the feeling.

MICHAEL: No, you don't! You don't know the feeling at all! You've never been in – a – a state of – desperation. Ever! You've never been at a point where everything is – absolutely – hopeless. Your life is smooth, and calm – and – and *easy*!

TERRY looks at him, shakes his head, sadly.

OK, OK, maybe not easy exactly, not now, not now your father's just – but generally. Generally your life is – well – easier than mine, anyhow.

TERRY: Everybody thinks my life is easy. I smile graciously, and entertain, and spend money like water, and everybody thinks 'good old Terry, not a care in the world – it's all so easy for him. Privileged upbringing, doing what he wants, scribbling away with the world at his feet – yes, it's so easy. It all just falls into place for him. He doesn't have to twitch a muscle'.

MICHAEL: Well. Compared to some others. Compared to some…

TERRY: They think writing plays is easy too. They just flow from the pen, in between rounds of golf, and emerge, fully-fledged, like little gems. All I have to do is get them typed up and sent off, and another load of cash comes rolling in. It's so unfair, they think. Why can't I be like that? I'm sure I could write something just as good as his stuff if only I tried. Oh, Midget, I know what people think. And I had thought that you weren't like that. I had thought that you were different. You could see the – the pain, the self-searching, the – the – yes, the self-loathing, too – that goes into it.

MICHAEL: Self-loathing?

TERRY: Yes! I hate some of the things I am! I hate some of the things I write, the characters I shape from – from personal experience – from my own friends, my family – but I can't help it. It's where it all comes from. It's what's in me. My own twisted little… I want to go beyond that. To write about a great character, a great life – examine it, explain it – I don't want to spend my life rooting around in my own feelings, my own personal…

He leaves the sentence hanging, takes a large gulp of brandy.

But you don't understand. After all.

Pause.

MICHAEL: I can try. *(A beat.)* I want to try. I do. Truly.

Pause.

Let me try. Your work is the most important thing. I want to help you with your work.

Pause. Lightly touches his sleeve.

I love you.

TERRY: Do you?

He nods.

Perhaps we have a future. Perhaps this is an auspicious year. A new Queen on the throne, and a new lover. How very neat.

MICHAEL playfully takes his hand and kisses it, in mock regal style.

Lights fade. MICHAEL leaves. YOUNGER TERRY remains.

Music.

SCENE THREE. 1959.

Little Court, Sunningdale. Late afternoon.

OLDER TERRY: In 1956 I was an extremely successful playwright. Not to mention the films. And suddenly the whole Royal Court thing exploded, and Coward, Priestley and I were all dismissed, sacked by the critics. Three years later I still couldn't understand it.

I wanted to be the English Chekhov. I admit it. No one thought I came close.

TERRY: And you simply couldn't face failure. Could you?

OLDER TERRY's expression clouds over. YOUNGER TERRY leaves.

From this point on, OLDER TERRY takes over as the centre of the drama. He unties his bow tie, discards his dinner jacket. Puts on a rumpled cardigan.

OLDER TERRY: I keep seeing visions. Faces – voices – torment me. I can see and hear one now, still, after all this time. It's not my father. It's a man I admired greatly. A leader. A hero. I want to discover what it was like to be him. I have never done anything heroic. I was a hero of a kind for a while at Harrow, in my cricketing days, but so was my father, so was my brother. That kind of petty, boyish heroism is nothing. I could never lead men against the odds in battle, rally them to my cause, convince them of their own bravery. I want to know what it is like to have that fire, that conviction, that…genius.

A figure appears out of the darkness. It is MICHAEL.

(Still to himself.) Who are you? I must find out who you are. What kind of man you are –

MICHAEL: *(Levelly.)* It's Michael.

OLDER TERRY: Michael…

MICHAEL: Midget.

OLDER TERRY: Oh. Yes… Midget.

MICHAEL: Who were you talking to?

OLDER TERRY: Oh…no one. I was…working. Thinking. Remembering.

The lights brighten.

MICHAEL: You were being very noisy about it.

OLDER TERRY: Was I?

MICHAEL: The Ugly Sisters are here.

OLDER TERRY: Hm?

MICHAEL: Freddie and Cuthbert.

OLDER TERRY: Oh? Already?

MICHAEL: They're always early. You invite them for six, and they'll turn up at 5.30. You invite them for ten and they –

OLDER TERRY: Yes, yes, I get the picture, Midget. Did I invite them?

MICHAEL: Probably. You usually do, and if you don't, they assume you have anyway.

OLDER TERRY: What time is it?

MICHAEL: It's cocktail time, of course. They've been to the Ivy for lunch and you are their next stop.

OLDER TERRY: Oh God. I don't think I'm up to that kind of evening. Can't you make them go away?

FREDDIE and CUTHBERT roll in, in very good humour. They are both a little older, but FREDDIE in particular is no less exuberant.

FREDDIE: Did you hear that, Cuthy? Mrs Rattigan CBE wants us to go away!

CUTHBERT: We can't do that. It's far too early to go away.

FREDDIE: And we've gone to all this trouble to get here.

CUTHBERT: Turned down several other invitations –

FREDDIE: Oh, lots. Lots of other offers, from lots of lovely people.

CUTHBERT: But we turned them all down, Terry.

FREDDIE: Yes, turned them all down, man and boy, all in favour of you, ducky, you and your lovely CBE. Aren't you the lucky one?

OLDER TERRY: Michael, you'd better warn the new cook that there will be four of us for supper.

MICHAEL: Are you sure? You don't have to, you know.

FREDDIE: Hark at her, Miss Sourpuss.

MICHAEL: I had rather hoped we'd have a quiet evening in for once.

FREDDIE: Some hope of that, rentboy.

MICHAEL: *(Rounding on him.)* Now if you start on me again –

FREDDIE: You'll thcream and you'll thcream and you'll thcream! And we'll all be so terrified, won't we, Cuthy? So terrified you'll flounce off and pretend to throw yourself under a passing Rolls-Royce.

MICHAEL: You're such a fucking asshole!

FREDDIE: No, dear, that's your job. Is there the remotest chance of any hospitality here, Terry – or do I have to walk to the drinks cabinet myself?

OLDER TERRY: All right, all right. Let's calm ourselves down and Michael will get you a drink.

MICHAEL: I certainly will not.

FREDDIE: Come on, Midget, play the game. You know you love being subservient.

MICHAEL: You have absolutely no respect for anybody, do you? You think you're so amusing.

FREDDIE: And most people agree with me. I offer a little passing entertainment wherever I go.

OLDER TERRY: I don't know how Rodney puts up with you after all these years.

FREDDIE: Rodney has no personality of his own, so he revels in mine.

OLDER TERRY: Very generous of you, my dear.

FREDDIE: A girl could die of thirst in this house. Actually, literally curl up and die right in the middle of the Persian rug.

MICHAEL: Then what are you waiting for?

OLDER TERRY sighs, goes to the drinks cabinet, proceeds to pour two large scotches.

CUTHBERT: I met someone quite interesting the other day. At a concert in St John's Smith Square.

He looks at them for a sign of interest.

FREDDIE: Fascinating.

CUTHBERT: One day I'll surprise you, Freddie.

FREDDIE: Nothing you do would surprise me, dear. I can read you like a book, and a dull one at that.

CUTHBERT: One day I'll meet someone rather wonderful.

FREDDIE: Not in that suit you won't.

MICHAEL: OK, OK, enough! Before you barged in here, Terry and I were having a serious talk. And you have completely ruined the moment.

FREDDIE: Oh, well, we're very sorry, aren't we, Cuthbert? We are contrite. Mary Mary, quite contrite.

CUTHBERT: Sorry, Terry.

OLDER TERRY hands drinks to CUTHBERT and FREDDIE.

OLDER TERRY: Michael is quite right. I am not in the mood for you two tonight. Especially not after one of your four-hour lunches.

MICHAEL goes up close to him and speaks with venom.

MICHAEL: Are you listening, asshole?

FREDDIE: *(Acidly.)* Give us a kiss, rentboy.

MICHAEL raises a hand as if to strike him.

OLDER TERRY: *(A warning.)* Michael.

MICHAEL stops, turns aside petulantly.

(Out front.) I miss dear Chips. He would have known how to help me. I want to be with my characters – and my beloved Puccini – and I'm saddled with these three. *(To CUTHBERT and FREDDIE.)* I am not feeling very well, my dears, so please behave, or I shall have to ask you to go.

CUTHBERT: Of course, Terry. Absolutely.

FREDDIE: Is it a touch of the Osbornes?

OLDER TERRY checks FREDDIE's expression to see if he is sending him up, decides that he isn't.

OLDER TERRY: It's not Osborne. It's not any of them. It's Aunt Edna.

FREDDIE: Who?

OLDER TERRY: Aunt Edna. She's deserted me.

FREDDIE: *(To CUTHBERT.)* What's he talking about?

CUTHBERT: It's an article he wrote. Aunt Edna represents his typical audience.

FREDDIE: *(Bemused.)* Really?

CUTHBERT: And Terry thinks his audience is now turning against him.

FREDDIE: *(To TERRY.)* Well, why worry, dear, when you've got all that money rolling in from the movies?

OLDER TERRY: That isn't the point.

FREDDIE: A hundred thousand dollars for the rights to *The Sleeping Prince*! That's more money than most people see in a lifetime! And from Miss Monroe's own pocket –

OLDER TERRY: Freddie, if you're going to start quoting dollars at me I shall go to bed for a week.

FREDDIE: Just get things in proportion, dear. That's all I'm saying.

OLDER TERRY: It's very far from *all* you're saying. It's your usual, thinly disguised, vulgar and rather spiteful envy.

FREDDIE: All right, I'm envious! Who wouldn't be?

CUTHBERT: *(Changing the subject.)* But at least you're working on something, Terry. That's excellent news. Excellent.

OLDER TERRY: I decided to take your advice, Cuthy.

CUTHBERT: *(Pleased.)* Oh?

OLDER TERRY: I'm not done with Lawrence. The film may have fallen through, but I have to write him. I can't let him go. So, as you kindly suggested, I'm trying to turn my film script into a stage play.

CUTHBERT: Excellent. It's a wonderful subject.

OLDER TERRY: But a large one. Very large indeed, full of endless desert, and hordes of Turkish soldiers and Bedouin tribesmen, and man at the pinnacle of his achievement as well as the depths of his despair. It would really work better as a film.

FREDDIE: I heard that David Lean is doing one now with some chap called Peter O'Toole. The name probably explains the casting.

OLDER TERRY: *(Muttering.)* My Lawrence. My hero. My idea.

FREDDIE: You should get Dirk Bogarde for the stage version, Terry. He's very box office. I could direct it for you. Mind you, I'd need a decent percentage –

OLDER TERRY: *(Ignoring him.)* Lawrence is doing his best to help me.

MICHAEL quietly gets up and pours a drink.

CUTHBERT: You mean Professor Lawrence, his brother?

OLDER TERRY: No. I mean Lawrence.

CUTHBERT: Lawrence himself?

OLDER TERRY: Who knows the secrets of human achievement better than he? He wants to be portrayed on stage. He wants to help me. *(Quoting.)* 'What is wrong in trying to write my name in history? Lawrence of Akaba perhaps – who knows?'

FREDDIE and CUTHBERT exchange looks.

CUTHBERT: But, Terry... Lawrence has been dead for years.

OLDER TERRY: *(As if to a simpleton.)* I know that.

MICHAEL hands the drink to OLDER TERRY.

Shouldn't be drinking this.

MICHAEL: It'll settle your stomach.

OLDER TERRY drinks.

OLDER TERRY: He communicates with me.

FREDDIE: How does he do that?

OLDER TERRY: In Morse code.

FREDDIE and CUTHBERT again exchange looks.

MICHAEL: Terry is convinced that the noises he hears in the night are messages from Lawrence. In Morse code.

FREDDIE: Really?

CUTHBERT: Oh my God...

OLDER TERRY: Clearly. Clearly he's trying to get through to me. He appears in my head sometimes, but he can't always do that. Or, rather, I can't. I can't always...locate him. Pin him down. He's a bit of a slippery customer is Lawrence.

MICHAEL: I've explained to Terry that in my opinion it's just the hot water pipes expanding and contracting –

OLDER TERRY: In your opinion.

MICHAEL: Yes, in my opinion. I said.

OLDER TERRY: He's trying to help me. Trying to tell me what's inside his head.

FREDDIE and CUTHBERT look at him in silence, all signs of drunkenness gone.

He discovered himself, you see. The sort of man he really was. It was something he had tried to conceal, or half knew, half feared, but had never acknowledged. He was forced to confront himself. *(Intensely)* What *I* have to discover is how that knowledge affected his will to achieve, and to be the great man he outwardly became. That's what I need to know.

CUTHBERT: *(Gently.)* Terry…are we talking about Lawrence now, or about yourself?

OLDER TERRY looks at them blankly. His mind is elsewhere.

OLDER TERRY: Hm?

FREDDIE: I know this might not be the moment to ask, my dear, but how is that musical version of *French Without Tears* coming along? You are still working on it?

CUTHBERT: Freddie, for God's sake!

FREDDIE: Well, I'm sorry, but I need to know! We said we'd ask Terry about it tonight, and so I have.

OLDER TERRY wanders to the drinks cabinet, contemplates the thought of another drink.

It's been promised for ages, Cuthbert, and the opening night is already scheduled. I need to start making plans.

MICHAEL: For once, Freddie, I agree with you.

FREDDIE: You do?

MICHAEL: Yes. I agree with your initial comment that this is *not the moment to ask*!

FREDDIE: *(Hushed voice.)* Is he all right? Should he see a doctor?

MICHAEL: Why?

FREDDIE: What do you mean, *why*?

MICHAEL: Do you want him to see a doctor for his own sake, or for yours?

OLDER TERRY turns and looks at them.

OLDER TERRY: I've changed my mind about supper. You can both bugger off.

FREDDIE looks stupefied.

I mean it. I've had enough.

FREDDIE: We've only just got here –

CUTHBERT: Come on, Freddie.

FREDDIE: Well, really. I only said he ought to see a doctor.

They leave, ushered out by MICHAEL.

OLDER TERRY: I warned you. I told you!

MICHAEL: *(Seeing them off.)* Bye bye.

OLDER TERRY sees YOUNGER TERRY on the opposite side of the stage. YOUNGER TERRY is holding the large scrapbook of press cuttings.

OLDER TERRY: *(To YOUNGER TERRY.)* What are you staring at?

YOUNGER TERRY smiles, indicates a page in the scrapbook.

Freddie nagged me into it! A musical version of *French Without Tears. (Ruefully.)* I even restored its original title, *Joie de Vivre.*

TERRY: And it closed after four performances, having been booed off the stage on the first night. The biggest disaster of your career.

OLDER TERRY: Why did I do it?

TERRY: Because everyone told you it was a surefire hit. Because everyone told you what you wanted to hear.

OLDER TERRY: Freddie was heart-broken. He'd been convinced it would secure his position as a director of consequence.

TERRY: Quite a miscalculation.

OLDER TERRY: As it was, he virtually denied he'd had anything to do with it, laying most of the blame on me.

TERRY: That's friendship for you.

OLDER TERRY: My play about Lawrence, though – that was a respectable success, wasn't it?

TERRY: Alec Guinness was in fine form.

OLDER TERRY: I knew it was what Lawrence himself wanted. He and I were at one. He showed me that in order to tell the truth, one has to undergo torment. I couldn't tell the truth about myself, but I could a very similar truth about Lawrence.

YOUNGER TERRY walks toward OLDER TERRY and looks him closely in the eye. Touches his cheek, momentarily.

TERRY: Is it such a torment? Having been me?

YOUNGER TERRY hands him the book of cuttings and goes.

Music.

SCENE FOUR. 1965.

TERRY's flat in Eaton Square, Belgravia. Night.

OLDER TERRY is poring over his scrapbook of press cuttings. There is an almost empty decanter of brandy on the floor and an empty glass. He has worked himself into a barely suppressed rage. MICHAEL is standing, watching him.

OLDER TERRY: Dear Mr Tynan…I hoped to reach you in time to stop you wasting your space on *Joie de Vivre* which, as you will know, closed on Saturday. I wish I had succeeded because I am a well-wisher of yours – although I recognise that the feeling is hardly reciprocated. Why – oh why – are you so boorishly abusive? And so…so dull and ill-tempered and…ideological. So you didn't like the show. Neither did 95 per cent of your colleagues. But none of them expressed their dislike one tenth as boorishly as you.

Why couldn't you just have said 'I hated the whole thing and left halfway through', and left it at that?

(Turning to MICHAEL.) Well? Come on – answer me!

He thrusts the scrapbook at MICHAEL.

MICHAEL: *(As the voice of Tynan.)* 'I really don't know why you put up with me. There must be moments when you wonder whether it's all worthwhile.'

OLDER TERRY: Speak up. Can't hear you.

MICHAEL: *(Louder, reading from the scrapbook)* 'I'm sorry you find me "dull and ill-tempered and ideological". I've tried being sparkling and good-tempered and mindless, and it doesn't seem to work. And isn't there, by the way, a trace of kettle-calling in your charges?'

OLDER TERRY: Yes, there was a trace of kettle-calling in my letter! I was in a flaming temper!

MICHAEL: Must we do this, Terry?

OLDER TERRY: *(Ignoring him.)* You seem to think you have the right to criticise a play for not being the play you want it to be. What do you know about writing plays, Mr Tynan? Have you ever tried it?

MICHAEL looks sadly at OLDER TERRY.

Come on, answer me back!

MICHAEL: 'No, Mr Rattigan, I have not tried it! Unlike you, I am aware of my limitations.'

OLDER TERRY: That's better. That's more like it! And what did you say about my Lawrence play? Go on! Don't just stand there. Let's hear it!

MICHAEL: *(Reciting.)* 'My main objection is not that its view of history is petty and blinkered –

OLDER TERRY: More precision!

MICHAEL: *(Overdoing it now.)* – what clinches my distaste is its verbal aridity, its flatness of phrase and – above all – its pat reliance on the same antithetical device in moments of crisis.'

MICHAEL hands the scrapbook back.

OLDER TERRY: Oh, you and your 'distaste'! Verbal aridity? Christ, you are a sanctimonious prick. And, as if heaping your bile on my plays weren't enough, you then turn film critic and heap even more bile on my screenplays! Is it because you hate my kind of writing, or is it my sexuality that so disturbs you? Yours is hardly conventional, Mr Tynan!

Why pick on me? That's all I want to know.

(A self-pitying wail.) Why?

MICHAEL moves away. OLDER TERRY seems to have exhausted himself, but then launches into another rant, shouting after him.

You think I'm obsessive? Yes, my friends think so too. I *am* obsessed. I am a man obsessed by his own fate. Viciously cast aside by…by pseudo-intellectuals who never see fit to…to evaluate a body of work with any vestige of…of… *balance.* Whose writing style is always to go for the jugular. How have I so offended you? How many more kicks in the teeth do you want to give me? What more do you want? A signed statement saying I'll never write again? Would that do it? Would that satisfy you?

He hurls the book of press cuttings to the floor and sinks back into his chair.

Lights up on CUTHBERT and MICHAEL, who are observing him in the shadows. The time of day is indeterminate – no daylight is apparent.

CUTHBERT: *(His voice more breathless now.)* How often does he get like this?

MICHAEL: Most weekdays.

CUTHBERT: And he keeps himself to himself?

MICHAEL: Locked away in the apartment, drinking, endlessly poring over his press cuttings, staring wildly into space.

CUTHBERT: And what do you think is happening?

MICHAEL: He's reliving his old arguments.

CUTHBERT: With his friends?

MICHAEL: Sometimes. Mostly critics, though. And mostly Kenneth Tynan.

CUTHBERT: Ah well. Yes. His bête noir. Does he talk to you about it?

MICHAEL: Oh yes. Sometimes I have to be Tynan.

CUTHBERT: You have to – ?

MICHAEL: Be Tynan for him. I play the part. Read out his reviews, his personal letters to Terry.

CUTHBERT: And then Terry responds?

MICHAEL: Exactly. He relives it all. Sometimes word for word.

CUTHBERT: Oh dear. Dear oh dear. Does he sleep much?

MICHAEL: Some nights hardly at all. Other nights he stays up late and goes to bed at about five in the morning. Sleeps right through the day.

CUTHBERT: Can I speak to him?

MICHAEL: Be my guest.

CUTHBERT goes to TERRY, pulls up a chair and sits beside him.

CUTHBERT: Hello old friend.

TERRY slowly takes in his presence.

It's Cuthbert. Old Cuthy. How are you?

OLDER TERRY: Cuthy…

CUTHBERT: Yes. How are you feeling?

OLDER TERRY: I'm not especially well. I think. I get these… pains. Sometimes.

CUTHBERT: What sort of pains, Terry?

OLDER TERRY: What?

CUTHBERT: What sort of pains do you get?

Pause.

OLDER TERRY: Not…pains. Exactly. I don't know. I…

CUTHBERT: Yes?

OLDER TERRY: I just think I'm…

A beat.

CUTHBERT: What? What are you?

OLDER TERRY: Tired, mostly.

CUTHBERT puts a hand on TERRY's arm.

And how are *you?*

CUTHBERT: Oh, you know me. The emphysema's not getting any better, but I survive.

OLDER TERRY: Something else is wrong, Cuthy. What is it?

CUTHBERT: No, no. Nothing wrong.

MICHAEL: I think it's time you rested now, Terry.

OLDER TERRY: Why?

MICHAEL: Well… You just said. You're tired.

OLDER TERRY: I'm not tired *now.* Why do you nanny me so much?

MICHAEL: You need looking after.

OLDER TERRY: You treat me like a child. You know that?

MICHAEL: No, I –

OLDER TERRY: Like a stupid child. You mollycoddle me.

CUTHBERT: I'm not sure that's quite fair, Terry.

OLDER TERRY: What do you know about it? Why does everybody else always know best?

He stares at them both in turn. His gaze settles on MICHAEL.

I used to be like you once. I used to be…attractive. Witty. The life and soul of the party. Oh, look – there I am…

YOUNGER TERRY appears.

Look at me. There. Can you see?

CUTHBERT: What? See what?

OLDER TERRY: Me. So handsome and debonair. The Best Dressed Man in London.

He holds his arms out. YOUNGER TERRY slowly approaches. OLDER TERRY gets up and tries to embrace him.

What do you think of me now, eh? I've still got life in me yet!

YOUNGER TERRY pushes him gently but firmly back into his chair, looks at him with something like contempt.

TERRY: I can't bear to look at you.

YOUNGER TERRY disappears.

OLDER TERRY gives an anguished cry, which he half stifles.

CUTHBERT: What is it? *(No response.)* Who are you talking to, Terry?

MICHAEL: Don't mind him. He gets like this sometimes. It passes.

CUTHBERT: Is there anything I can do?

MICHAEL: No.

CUTHBERT: I hate to see him like this. It's as if – *(He stops.)*

MICHAEL: He's not losing his mind.

CUTHBERT: No, no, I didn't think –

MICHAEL: There's just a lot of stuff in there. Past history. Relationships, plays, family stuff. He just has to sort through it all, in his own way.

CUTHBERT: I see.

MICHAEL: It's all quite real to him at the time, but then he forgets. And we have to do it all over again.

CUTHBERT: Poor old thing.

MICHAEL: He's still bright as a button in between times.

CUTHBERT: Well, that's encouraging.

MICHAEL: He's got it into his head to chase after some new young playwright, so he can't be all that ill. He's backed him financially too.

CUTHBERT: Oh yes?

OLDER TERRY: It's Joe Orton. Michael is extremely jealous of him.

MICHAEL: No, I didn't say that –

OLDER TERRY: You didn't have to.

CUTHBERT: Well, I'd better…leave you to it.

OLDER TERRY: I invest in talent where I see it. Which is why I've also invested in Michael's interior design business.

CUTHBERT: Ah.

OLDER TERRY: Was there something you wanted to say, Cuthbert?

CUTHBERT: No, no… Well…

OLDER TERRY: Some reason for coming round?

CUTHBERT: I came round to see you, Terry.

OLDER TERRY: You've been a bit of a stranger of late.

CUTHBERT: Yes, I… Well, you haven't been well, and what with one thing and another…

OLDER TERRY: Out with it, Cuthy.

Pause.

CUTHBERT: All right. I've lost my job on the *New Statesman*. I am no longer a literary critic.

OLDER TERRY: My dear, I'm so sorry. Not because you've been defending me, I hope?

CUTHBERT: *(Smiles.)* No, I'm sure not.

OLDER TERRY: And how is…everything else?

CUTHBERT: The same as usual.

OLDER TERRY: On your own again?

CUTHBERT: I'm afraid so.

OLDER TERRY: Michael, we must do something to help.

MICHAEL: What did you have in mind?

OLDER TERRY: That house in Brighton you're so desperate to buy – make all the arrangements and Cuthy can live there for a while. Till he gets himself sorted out.

MICHAEL: What about you? Us?

OLDER TERRY: We can have a few parties at the weekends, but I shall hate the house, I know. I hate the flat you bought in Embassy Court, and I shall hate the house as well, but never mind. It'll give you some interior designing to do, and it'll give Cuthy a place to stay. What do you say, Cuthy?

CUTHBERT: Well, I…

OLDER TERRY: Just don't tell Freddie. Not yet anyway. Or he'll be down there before you can say manly buttocks. Never give you a moment's peace.

CUTHBERT: *(Overcome.)* Terry, I…

OLDER TERRY: Ssh. It's done. Enough. I'm tired. Off you go.

CUTHBERT gives him a clumsy hug. He goes.

MICHAEL: I'll see you out.

MICHAEL follows him. OLDER TERRY remains in his chair.

A slightly strange piece of music is heard.

A middle-aged lady appears and quietly seats herself next to OLDER TERRY. She is dressed in a rather drab, but certainly not cheap, outfit. Blouse, jacket, three-quarter length skirt, sensible shoes. She wears glasses and her hair is neatly tied into a bun. She is also wearing an unflattering hat and a pair of gloves, which she removes with some care after she has sat down. She is AUNT EDNA.

OLDER TERRY has so far given no sign of recognition or acknowledgement. There is a momentary silence between them.

He reaches down for the decanter and brandy glass and pours himself a drink. He then looks at her and proffers the decanter.

AUNT EDNA: No, thank you. I only drink at Christmas, weddings and funerals. And then only a glass of dry sherry.

TERRY drains his glass.

That stuff can kill you, you know.

OLDER TERRY: But it's not the stuff that *will* kill me.

He pours and drinks again.

I'm sorry. I'm feeling a little...under the weather.

AUNT EDNA: Is that what you call it?

He gives her a quizzical look as if to detect her tone.

So this is your palatial apartment. Very impressive, I must say.

OLDER TERRY: Thank you.

AUNT EDNA: But then you've always lived in very elegant surroundings, haven't you? At smart addresses. Albany, Chester Square. Sunningdale.

OLDER TERRY: I like to play golf of an afternoon.

AUNT EDNA: Quite so. And here you are back in London. Eaton Square no less. My my. You do get around.

OLDER TERRY: Aunt Edna...are you criticising me?

AUNT EDNA: Good heavens, no. Where a man chooses to live is entirely his own business. But I like to think that your financial success is not entirely unconnected with myself.

OLDER TERRY: No indeed. I have much to thank you for.

AUNT EDNA: Nevertheless, you blame me for your misfortunes. For your declining popularity.

OLDER TERRY: Have I ever said as much?

AUNT EDNA: My name has frequently been taken in vain in the newspapers. Bandied about in *The Observer* and suchlike. Particularly by that Mr Tynan.

OLDER TERRY: Ah, him. Yes. Kenneth Tight-arse.

AUNT EDNA: Please, Mr Rattigan. Language.

OLDER TERRY: I'm so sorry. I was forgetting myself.

AUNT EDNA: There were others who took my name in vain too. The name you yourself gave me. Aunt Edna indeed. Far too cosy and twee.

OLDER TERRY: Yes, I'm afraid I misjudged things as far as you are concerned.

AUNT EDNA: We all make mistakes, Mr Rattigan. Sometimes we own up to them. And sometimes we compound them by protesting too much.

OLDER TERRY: I only protested when I saw injustice.

AUNT EDNA: Yes yes yes. Injustice. Doing right. That's what your *Winslow Boy* play was all about, wasn't it?

OLDER TERRY: Yes.

AUNT EDNA: I enjoyed that.

OLDER TERRY: Thank you.

AUNT EDNA: One of your best.

OLDER TERRY: Well, it was written for you.

AUNT EDNA: Of course. I personified your audience. 'A nice, respectable, middle-class, middle-aged maiden lady with time on her hands and the money to help her pass it.' Those were your words, Mr Rattigan. Your description of me. Well, here I am.

OLDER TERRY: Here you are.

AUNT EDNA: But look at me, Mr Rattigan. I am not an inspiring figure. I am allowed no children, no husband, I exist in a vacuum – the only creation you never put on a stage. And now I have come to tell you what I think.

OLDER TERRY: I assume I'm not going to like it.

AUNT EDNA: I have been faithful to you over the years. I have served you well.

OLDER TERRY: You have.

AUNT EDNA: But I have to tell you that you had it coming.

OLDER TERRY: What?

AUNT EDNA: Your reversal in fortune. *(A beat.)* It's not that you stopped being a good writer, you understand. I actually liked *Joie de Vivre*. It was rather fun.

OLDER TERRY: Thank you. No one else thought so.

AUNT EDNA: The problem is not your writing. The problem is you.

TERRY looks at her sharply.

You loved your own success too much.

OLDER TERRY: I earned my success!

AUNT EDNA: Yes, and then there was a war, Mr Rattigan. And attitudes changed.

OLDER TERRY: I did my bit in the war –

AUNT EDNA: Oh yes. You did your bit. But as soon as it was all over, you carried on with your playboy lifestyle – I'm sorry, but there's no other word for it – and you grandly assumed you could swan about as you had before and everybody would still applaud you for it. Your plays were expensively mounted, and beautifully dressed, but they didn't acknowledge that the world had moved on. The upper and middle classes were no longer all the rage.

OLDER TERRY: Well, more's the pity.

AUNT EDNA: And that leads me to my next point. Against any kind of better judgement, you went into print at the slightest opportunity to defend yourself, and to complain bitterly that you were misunderstood, and maligned. It wasn't an attractive display, Mr Rattigan. It made you look spoiled, as indeed you were. And supercilious. Which you also were. And the new young writers had a field day. You set yourself up and they knocked you down. I'm sorry to be so candid but, as you know, I always speak my mind. I know what I like, and sometimes I find that I can like some rather unexpected things. And I don't like to have my judgement, and my taste, called into question. *Waiting for Godot* is a very strange play in many ways, but it is also beautiful. And yet you dared to assume that I would hate it. Shame on you. And as for your last effort, in 1963 – a very unsavoury piece. *Man and Boy* indeed. A man pimping his own son? Really, Mr Rattigan.

OLDER TERRY: Pimping?

AUNT EDNA: Oh yes, I know the word. You needn't think I don't. And now, having said my piece, I shall take my leave.

She stands.

OLDER TERRY: No, wait! Aunt Edna, please. Tell me one thing. One thing I…desperately need to know.

AUNT EDNA: What is that?

OLDER TERRY: My play *Separate Tables* –

AUNT EDNA: Ah, the seaside hotel – yes –

OLDER TERRY: Did you understand what it was really about? The character of the Major, I mean? His weakness – accosting young women in cinemas –

AUNT EDNA: I think I did, Mr Rattigan. It was about one of life's unfortunates. A man who cannot control his sexual urges. A deviant personality.

OLDER TERRY: Yes, yes, but did you understand what his offence really was, Aunt Edna?

AUNT EDNA: You've just told me. Accosting young women.

OLDER TERRY: No, no! I had to write that because otherwise the play wouldn't have got past the Lord Chamberlain. Did you feel that I was hinting at something else?

AUNT EDNA: I didn't think there was very much hinting at all. The man was a pervert.

OLDER TERRY: *(Persisting.)* The Major was really concealing a different secret altogether. A different kind of desire. If that version had been performed I might have achieved something lasting! Something truly worthwhile.

AUNT EDNA: We English are pretty tolerant on the whole, Mr Rattigan, but too much talk of unnatural desires, and pimping and whatnot, and we get uncomfortable. I'm sorry if that's not what you wanted me to say.

She puts on her gloves.

You should have forgotten me, you know. You used me to your advantage, and then you hated it when others used me against you. It was as if you were condemning yourself out of your own mouth. But I wish you well, Mr Rattigan. Sincerely I do. I know that you have a great play in you yet.

OLDER TERRY: You do?

AUNT EDNA: Oh yes. You've just got to keep yourself well enough to complete it. And sober enough. You really must do something about your drinking, you know. It's most unattractive. Your mother would have said exactly the same, I'm sure. I wish you good day.

She disappears. The music echoes, faintly, again.

A look of pain passes over his face. He gropes for his scrapbook and holds it with care.

Spot on YOUNGER TERRY watching him from the sidelines.

OLDER TERRY slowly puts down his scrapbook and stands, with some difficulty. He makes his way towards YOUNGER TERRY. Stares at him, pleadingly, his arm reaching as if to touch him.

TERRY: Believe in your ghosts, if you will, old man. But we can't help you now.

YOUNGER TERRY slides away into darkness and OLDER TERRY stands in his place, which is also the same position in which he started the play.

Lights fade around him.

Music.

SCENE FIVE. EPILOGUE. 1977.

We are back in the blank space which is about to become the Royal Box at Her Majesty's Theatre, Haymarket.

OLDER TERRY: Can one make sense of the life one has lived? Can it be revised and redrafted? Can one craft it, like a play? Give it structure, and thus meaning? Craftsmanship was a word that became a term of abuse as far as I was concerned. Why? Because it signified something too controlled, too restrained? Too mechanical? All easy assumptions. But wrong. The drama was embodied in my craftsmanship! And they turned my strengths against me. Tried to teach me a lesson in humility.

Perhaps I deserved it. Perhaps Aunt Edna was right.

Should I be sorry for the way I have lived? Should I be *sorry* for being what I am?

Our later years are a bitch. So little time left and we agonise over what has gone before. We want to package it up like a suitcase to take into the afterlife. If we can just shape it to fit this suitcase then we can die happy. And then we can stop fretting over what they will say of us when we are gone. We have to take our suitcase and say 'This is me. This is my life. It is what it is – I have done my best to understand it – now you can say what you like.'

We conceal so much from each other and from ourselves. Even when declaring our feelings, if we ever do, we only reveal half the truth. Why? Self-protection? Possibly. Fear of rejection? Undoubtedly. And art. We practise the skill of the tightrope walker – verbally speaking – in order to be attractive, enticing, but we always know we have the safety net of concealment below us – and *that*, in time, becomes our own sense of self. The concealment becomes the thing itself.

Perhaps in that sense it destroys you. Destroys…me.

He gives a sudden grimace of pain.

Lights change. OLDER TERRY is recalling an earlier time.

MICHAEL appears at his side, dressed for the evening. Perhaps his hair is now a little grey at the temples.

MICHAEL: Terry?

OLDER TERRY: What is it?

MICHAEL: A cable has just arrived.

OLDER TERRY: A cable?

He hands OLDER TERRY a telegram. OLDER TERRY struggles to read it. Then gives a sudden gasp.

MICHAEL: I'm sorry, Terry.

OLDER TERRY: Oh God.

MICHAEL: He was a good friend to you.

OLDER TERRY: Yes. *(Pause.)* Oh God. *(Pause.)* Poor Cuthbert. Such a dear, dear man. *(Pause.)* I shall miss him, Midget.

He hands the telegram back to MICHAEL.

MICHAEL: Of course.

OLDER TERRY: *(Close to tears.)* He was sometimes…the only one who stood up for me. Championed me. Lost his job because of me.

MICHAEL: I know.

OLDER TERRY: Things won't be the same.

MICHAEL: No. *(A beat.)* But you've still got me.

Lights change again.

OLDER TERRY removes his cardigan. The space he is occupying is now the Royal Box. It is evening.

OLDER TERRY: And now I face my audience, and my critics, for the final time. Here I am, at the first night of my final play, in the Royal Box at Her Majesty's Theatre, Haymarket.

MICHAEL helps OLDER TERRY into his dinner jacket.

So many others are not here. My darling mama, my father, and many friends. No Binkie Beaumont, no Tony Goldschmidt, who was blown to pieces in the war, and – thank goodness – but only because he's decamped to the States – no Kenneth Tynan to take my play apart at the seams.

MICHAEL ties OLDER TERRY's bow tie for him.

Most of all, though…most of all, I miss dear Cuthbert. He did so much for me in his own quiet way and never asked for anything in return. We loved each other, of course, but never uttered a word on the subject. It was a simple, pure affection made manifest by a discreet glance in a roomful of screaming laughter. Cuthbert was a discreet man, a man who couldn't abide any fuss, but who would have defended me to the death. Which, in a sense, he did.

OLDER TERRY sits, in some discomfort. He gives another grimace of pain. MICHAEL reacts.

OLDER TERRY: I'm all right, Midget. *(He pats his hand.)* Relax.

MICHAEL: Are you talking to yourself again?

OLDER TERRY: I'm talking to the audience. The audience in here. *(Indicates his head.)* Revisiting a few old times. A few old memories. And a few recent ones.

MICHAEL: If I were you I'd concentrate on tonight.

OLDER TERRY: Yes. Quite right. For almost the first time in my life I am going to watch the whole performance of a West End opening night. No getting up and nipping into the bar now. And then we'll go home and let the critics do their worst.

MICHAEL: Back to the hospital, I think. That would be wisest.

Pause. We hear the background buzz of an audience assembling.

OLDER TERRY: Don't leave me.

MICHAEL: Why would I do that?

OLDER TERRY: Cuthbert and Freddie were wrong about you, Midget.

MICHAEL: I hope you always knew they were.

OLDER TERRY: Oh yes. But they meant well. Help me stand. I want to look at the audience.

He stands, painfully. MICHAEL assists him.

Yes. It's all right. The stalls are filling up nicely. Good. Good. We might stand half a chance.

He sits back down again, with great care. MICHAEL sits beside him.

I always hate this bit the most. The last moments before curtain up.

MICHAEL: I know.

OLDER TERRY: Wish me luck.

MICHAEL takes his hand. Gently raises it to his lips in a gesture reminiscent of his mock regal kiss at the end of Act 2 Scene 1.

They hold hands and wait. The buzz of the audience subsides. Light streams upwards over them as the 'curtain' rises. We see their transfixed faces for a few moments, held in a pin spot. Then:

Blackout. Silence.

WWW.OBERONBOOKS.COM

Follow us on www.twitter.com/@oberonbooks
& www.facebook.com/oberonbook